TASC Math Book
Study Guide

TASC Math Practice Questions and
Explanations for the Test Assessing
Secondary Completion

TABLE OF CONTENTS

INTRODUCTION

Congratulations on choosing to take the TASC! By purchasing this book, you've taken an important step on your path to earning your high school equivalency.

This guide will provide you with a detailed overview of the TASC, so you will know exactly what to expect on test day. We'll take you through all the concepts covered on the exam and give you the opportunity to test your knowledge with practice questions. Even if it's been a while since you last took a major test, don't worry; we'll make sure you're more than ready!

What is the TASC?

The Test Assessing Secondary Completion, or TASC, is a high school equivalency test—composed of five subtests—that certifies that the test-taker has high school-level academic skills. Fourteen states currently offer the TASC. You may take the subtests all together or individually, and you must pass all five subtests in order to pass the test overall. If a test-taker in one of those states passes the test, then he or she is eligible to receive a high school-equivalency diploma which can be used in job applications or in applying to colleges or universities. The test is specifically designed for individuals who did not earn a high school diploma, regardless of the reason.

What's on the TASC?

The TASC gauges high school-level content knowledge and skills in five areas: mathematics, reading, writing, science, and social studies. Candidates are expected to be able to read closely, write clearly, and solve quantitative, algebraic and geometric problems. You also must show strong content knowledge in life science, physical science, Earth and space science, civics and government, United States history, world history, economics, and geography.

The test includes a variety of questions, including multiple-choice, gridded response, constructed response, written prompt, stimuli-based, and technology-enhanced (i.e., computer-based) questions. The multiple-choice questions are a standard style in which the test-taker selects the best answer among a series of choices. For gridded response questions, the test taker must write his or her answer and then fill in the corresponding bubbles. Stimuli-based questions will provide the test-taker with a visual or a short reading which must be used to answer the question or series of questions which follow it. Technology-enhanced questions utilize computer-based methods—like dropping and dragging the correct answer or clicking on a specific area of an image—to answer questions. The written prompt will allow you to write an answer to a question in an open, blank area.

Each subtest is taken separately. You must complete one subtest before moving on to the next. You will have 105 minutes for the math test—divided into two periods (55 and 50 minutes respectively), 110 minutes for the writing test, 85 minutes for the reading test, 75 minutes for the science test, and 75 minutes for the social studies test.

What's on the TASC Exam?

MATHEMATICS

Subject	Percentage per Subject
Algebra	26%
Geometry	23%
Functions	26%
Numbers and quantity	13%
Statistics and probability	12%

Total	Number and Format of Questions
105 minutes	42 multiple-choice (computer-based)
	43 multiple-choice (paper-based)
	11 gridded-response
	1 constructed-response
	1 technology-enhanced (computer-based)

WRITING

Subject	Percentage per Subject
Writing	15%
Grammar/usage	30%
Capitalization/punctuation/spelling	25%
Knowledge of language	30%

Total	Number and Format of Questions
105 minutes (includes 45 minutes to write essay)	50 multiple-choice (computer-based)
	51 multiple-choice (paper-based)
	1 writing prompt based on 2 passages
	1 constructed-response item
	1 technology-enhanced item (computer-based)

READING LITERACY

Subject	Percentage per Subject
Reading informational texts	70%
Reading literature	30%

Total	Number and Format of Questions
75 minutes	48 multiple-choice (computer-based)
	49 multiple-choice (paper-based)
	up to 8 passages
	1 constructed-response item
	1 technology-enhanced item (computer-based)

Science

Subject	Percentage per Subject
Physical sciences	36%
Life sciences	36%
Earth and space science	28%

Total	Number and Format of Questions
85 minutes	48 multiple-choice (computer-based) 49 multiple-choice (paper-based) 8 stimuli 1 constructed-response 1 technology-enhanced (computer-based)

Social Studies

Subject	Percentage per Subject
US history	25%
World history	15%
Civics and government	25%
Geography	15%
Economics	20%

Total	Number and Format of Questions
75 minutes	48 multiple-choice (computer-based) 49 multiple-choice (paper-based) 8 stimuli 1 constructed-response 1 technology-enhanced (computer-based)

MATHEMATICS: The mathematics test assesses your understanding of core principles and concepts in algebra, geometry, and arithmetic. You will need to know how to create equations and inequalities involving multiple variables. You also must be able to graph those equations and inequalities and rearrange them in order to highlight particular quantities or solve problems. You also must be able to use and solve polynomials and build and interpret functions, including domain and range. Finally, you must understand basic geometric concepts, including measurement and triangles. You also must be able to use geometry to model concepts and solve real-world problems.

WRITING: The writing test assesses your mastery of standard English and your ability to express ideas in writing. You must be able to demonstrate a solid knowledge of grammar, including the function of phrases and clauses, the different types of sentences, the function of verbals (e.g., gerunds), the various forms and uses of verbs, and types of phrases. You also must demonstrate a strong knowledge of punctuation, capitalization, and spelling. Test-takers should be able to properly use commas, ellipses, semicolons, colons, hyphens, and dashes. You also must show that you have a strong vocabulary and can precisely choose the appropriate words to express your ideas clearly. Finally, you must be able to write arguments that support analysis of provided texts and support those arguments with specific and grounded evidence taken from the texts.

READING: The reading test assesses your ability to read and comprehend a variety of informational and literary texts. You must be able to read a text closely to determine what it is directly saying, which includes identifying key supporting details. Test-takers must also be able to draw logical inferences from a text and determine the central idea or theme of a text. You should then be able to analyze how that theme or idea is developed over the course of the text. The test will also assess your ability to analyze and interpret texts: the role of various individuals, events and ideas, the use of words and phrases, and the way in which the text is structured. Finally, you should be able to analyze how point of view impacts the content and style of a text.

SCIENCE: The science test assesses your understanding of content in the three major areas of science: Earth and space science, life science, and physical science. In Earth and space science, you should be able to understand the solar system, including the life cycles of the sun and stars, theories about the origin of the universe, and the basics of plate tectonics. You should also be able to use evidence and scientific reasoning to support arguments about the history of Earth and create a model detailing the internal structure of Earth. In addition, you will be asked about natural resources and the ways in which human activity has impacted our planet. For life sciences, you should understand the major processes and characteristics of multicellular organisms as well as how ecosystems function. You must also demonstrate a comprehension of cells, DNA, and chromosomes and how research has increased our understanding of their role in living organisms. For physical sciences, you should understand how to construct an experiment and model chemical reactions, as well as how the design of a chemical system impacts outcomes. You should also be able to explain energy conservation and conversion, motion, and momentum, and should have a firm grasp on key scientific laws, like Newton's laws and Coulomb's law.

SOCIAL STUDIES: The social studies test assesses your general understanding of history, government, economics, and geography. The emphasis of the test is on United States history, and civics and government. You should have a general knowledge of the major eras of American history, from the Revolution to the present day, with a particular focus on the Civil War and Reconstruction, the Great Depression and World War II, and the postwar United States. In civics, you will be asked to demonstrate a good understanding of American politics and government, the foundations of the American political system, and the role of citizens in the American democracy. You will also be tested on the values and principles of the Constitution and how the United States relates to other countries of the world. In addition, you should know the major themes and events of world history, from the beginnings of human society through the twentieth century. For geography, you should understand the five themes of geography, the different types of geographical systems, and how both humans and the environment can impact each other. Finally, you will need to demonstrate a solid comprehension of economics, especially micro- and macroeconomics and the government's role in the economic system.

How is the TASC Scored?

If you take the computer-based test, you will receive your TASC scores within twenty-four hours of completing the exam. If you take the paper-based test, you will receive your score within ten days of your test date.

Each subtest is scored separately, and each question is worth one raw point, with the exception of the written prompt of the writing test, which is scored independently. The total number of raw points earned on a subtest is then scaled to a score between 100 and 800. To pass a subtest, you must earn at least 500 scaled score points.

The written prompt in the writing test is worth 8 points. It is scored by two separate graders on a scale of 0 – 4. If the graders' scores vary by more than one point, then the final score is determined by a master grader. In order to pass the written prompt, you must receive at least two out of eight points.

There is no overall score for passing the TASC. Instead, you must pass each of the subtests and the written prompt.

There is no guessing penalty on the TASC exam, so you should always guess if you do not know the answer to a question.

How is the TASC Administered?

The TASC exam can be taken either as a computer-based test or a paper-based test at a wide range of sites in the states that accept the TASC for high school equivalency. To find a test center near you, check http://www.tasctest.com/test-center-locations-for-test-center-admins.html.

You will need to print your registration ticket from your online account and bring it, along with your identification, to the testing site on test day. Some test centers will require other forms or documentation, so make sure to check with your test center in advance. No pens, pencils, erasers, printed or written materials, electronic devices or calculators are allowed. If you are taking the computer-based version of the test, an online scientific calculator will be provided to you at the time of the test. If you are taking a paper-based test, you will be provided a handheld calculator. You may only use the calculator on the first part of the math test and on the science test. You will also receive a formula reference sheet for the math test. Check in advance with your state and testing center for specific testing guidelines, including restrictions on dress and accessories.

You may take the subtests all on the same day or individually on separate days. There is no required order for completing the test. Certain states may apply limits to the amount of time available for completing all five tests.

There are three versions of each test, so you may retake a subtest if you do not pass. However, it is recommended that you wait at least one month before retaking the test, and you may only retest three times in a calendar year. You will receive a different version of the test each time. If you still need to retake the test after a third attempt, you must wait sixty days. If you do not pass one subtest, you are not required to retake all of the tests—only the one you failed. However, you may not retake any subtest until you have taken each subtest at least once.

About This Guide

This guide will help you master the most important test topics and develop critical test-taking skills. We have built features into our books to prepare you for your tests and increase your score. Along with a detailed summary of the test's format, content, and scoring, we offer an in-depth overview of the content knowledge required to pass the test. In the review you'll find sidebars that provide interesting information, highlight key concepts, and review content so that you can solidify your understanding of the exam's concepts. You can also test your knowledge with sample questions throughout the text and practice questions that reflect the content and format of the TASC. We're pleased you've chosen Accepted, Inc. to be a part of your journey!

NUMBERS AND OPERATIONS

This chapter provides a review of the basic yet critical components of mathematics such as manipulating fractions, comparing numbers, and using units. These concepts will provide the foundation for more complex mathematical operations in later chapters.

Types of Numbers

Numbers are placed in categories based on their properties.

- A NATURAL NUMBER is greater than 0 and has no decimal or fraction attached. These are also sometimes called counting numbers {1, 2, 3, 4, ...}.

- WHOLE NUMBERS are natural numbers and the number 0 {0, 1, 2, 3, 4, ...}.

- INTEGERS include positive and negative natural numbers and 0 {..., –4, –3, –2, –1, 0, 1, 2, 3, 4, ...}.

- A RATIONAL NUMBER can be represented as a fraction. Any decimal part must terminate or resolve into a repeating pattern. Examples include –12, $-\frac{4}{5}$, 0.36, $7.\overline{7}$, $26\frac{1}{2}$, etc.

- An IRRATIONAL NUMBER cannot be represented as a fraction. An irrational decimal number never ends and never resolves into a repeating pattern. Examples include $-\sqrt{7}$, π, and 0.34567989135...

- A REAL NUMBER is a number that can be represented by a point on a number line. Real numbers include all the rational and irrational numbers.

- An IMAGINARY NUMBER includes the imaginary unit i, where $i = \sqrt{-1}$ Because $i^2 = -1$, imaginary numbers produce a negative value when squared. Examples of imaginary numbers include $-4i$, $0.75i$, $i\sqrt{2}$ and $\frac{8}{3}i$.

◆ A **COMPLEX NUMBER** is in the form $a + bi$, where a and b are real numbers. Examples of complex numbers include $3 + 2i$, $-4 + i$, $\sqrt{3} - i\sqrt[3]{5}$ and $\frac{5}{8} - \frac{7i}{8}$. All imaginary numbers are also complex.

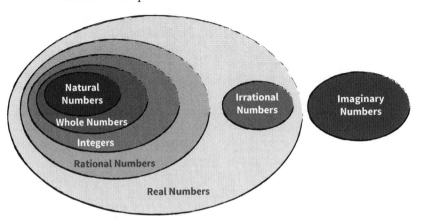

Figure 1.1. Types of Numbers

The **FACTORS** of a natural number are all the numbers that can multiply together to make the number. For example, the factors of 24 are 1, 2, 3, 4, 6, 8, 12, and 24. Every natural number is either prime or composite. A **PRIME NUMBER** is a number that is only divisible by itself and 1. (The number 1 is not considered prime.) Examples of prime numbers are 2, 3, 7, and 29. The number 2 is the only even prime number. A **COMPOSITE NUMBER** has more than two factors. For example, 6 is composite because its factors are 1, 6, 2, and 3. Every composite number can be written as a unique product of prime numbers, called the **PRIME FACTORIZATION** of the number. For example, the prime factorization of 90 is $90 = 2 \times 3^2 \times 5$. All integers are either even or odd. An even number is divisible by 2; an odd number is not.

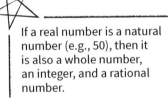

If a real number is a natural number (e.g., 50), then it is also a whole number, an integer, and a rational number.

Properties of Number Systems

A system is **CLOSED** under an operation if performing that operation on two elements of the system results in another element of that system. For example, the integers are closed under the operations of addition, subtraction, and multiplication but not division. Adding, subtracting, or multiplying two integers results in another integer. However, dividing two integers could result in a rational number that is not an integer $\left(-2 \div 3 = \frac{-2}{3}\right)$.

◆ The rational numbers are closed under all four operations (except for division by 0).

◆ The real numbers are closed under all four operations.

◆ The complex numbers are closed under all four operations.

- The irrational numbers are NOT closed under ANY of the four operations.

The **COMMUTATIVE PROPERTY** holds for an operation if order does not matter when performing the operation. For example, multiplication is commutative for integers: $(-2)(3) = (3)(-2)$.

The **ASSOCIATIVE PROPERTY** holds for an operation if elements can be regrouped without changing the result. For example, addition is associative for real numbers: $-3 + (-5 + 4) = (-3 + -5) + 4$.

The **DISTRIBUTIVE PROPERTY** of multiplication over addition allows a product of sums to be written as a sum of products: $a(b + c) = ab + ac$. The value a is distributed over the sum $(b + c)$. The acronym FOIL (First, Outer, Inner, Last) is a useful way to remember the distributive property.

When an operation is performed with an **IDENTITY ELEMENT** and another element a, the result is a. The identity element for multiplication on real numbers is 1 ($a \times 1 = a$), and for addition is 0 ($a + 0 = a$).

An operation of a system has an **INVERSE ELEMENT** if applying that operation with the inverse element results in the identity element. For example, the inverse element of a for addition is $-a$ because $a + (-a) = 0$. The inverse element of a for multiplication is $\frac{1}{a}$ because $a \times \frac{1}{a} = 1$.

EXAMPLES

1) Classify the following numbers as natural, whole, integer, rational, or irrational. (The numbers may have more than one classification.)

   A. 72

   B. $-\frac{2}{3}$

   C. $\sqrt{5}$

   Answers:

   A. The number is **natural**, **whole**, an **integer**, and **rational**.

   B. The fraction is **rational**.

   C. The number is **irrational**. (It cannot be written as a fraction, and written as a decimal is approximately 2.2360679...)

2) Determine the real and imaginary parts of the following complex numbers.

   A. 20

   B. $10 - i$

   C. $15i$

Answers:

A complex number is in the form of $a + bi$, where a is the real part and bi is the imaginary part.

A. $20 = 20 + 0i$
The real part is 20, and there is no imaginary part.

B. $10 - i = 10 - 1i$
The real part is 10, and $-1i$ is the imaginary part.

C. $15i = 0 + 15i$
The real part is 0, and the imaginary part is 15i.

3) Answer True or False for each statement:

A. The natural numbers are closed under subtraction.

B. The sum of two irrational numbers is irrational.

C. The sum of a rational number and an irrational number is irrational.

Answers:

A. is false. Subtracting the natural number 7 from 2 results in $2 - 7 = -5$, which is an integer, but not a natural number.

B. is false. For example, $(5 - 2\sqrt{3}) + (2 + 2\sqrt{3}) = 7$. The sum of two irrational numbers in this example is a whole number, which is not irrational. The sum of a rational number and an irrational number is sometimes rational and sometimes irrational.

C. is true. Because irrational numbers have decimal parts that are unending and with no pattern, adding a repeating or terminating decimal will still result in an unending decimal without a pattern.

4) Answer True or False for each statement:

A. The associative property applies for multiplication in the real numbers.

B. The commutative property applies to all real numbers and all operations.

Answers:

A. is true. For all real numbers, $a \times (b \times c) = (a \times b) \times c$. Order of multiplication does not change the result.

B. is false. The commutative property does not work for subtraction or division on real numbers. For example, $12 - 5 = 7$, but $5 - 12 = -7$ and $10 \div 2 = 5$, but $2 \div 10 = \frac{1}{5}$.

Operations with Complex Numbers

Operations with complex numbers are similar to operations with real numbers in that complex numbers can be added, subtracted, multiplied, and divided. When adding or subtracting, the imaginary parts and real parts are combined separately. When multiplying, the distributive property (FOIL) can be applied. Note that multiplying complex numbers often creates the value i^2 which can be simplified to −1.

To divide complex numbers, multiply both the top and bottom of the fraction by the COMPLEX CONJUGATE of the divisor (bottom number). The complex conjugate is the complex number with the sign of the imaginary part changed. For example, the complex conjugate of 3 + 4i would be 3 − 4i. Since both the top and the bottom of the fraction are multiplied by the same number, the fraction is really just being multiplied by 1. When simplified, the denominator of the fraction will now be a real number.

EXAMPLES

1) Simplify: $(3 − 2i) − (−2 + 8i)$

Answer:

$(3 − 2i) − (−2 + 8i)$	
$= (3 − 2i) − 1(−2 + 8i)$ $= 3 − 2i + 2 − 8i$	Distribute the −1.
$\mathbf{= 5 − 10i}$	Combine like terms.

2) Simplify: $\frac{4i}{(5 − 2i)}$

Answer:

$\frac{4i}{(5 − 2i)}$	
$= \frac{4i}{5 − 2i}\left(\frac{5 + 2i}{5 + 2i}\right)$ $= \frac{20i + 8i^2}{25 + 10i − 10i − 4i^2}$	Multiply the top and bottom of the fraction by the complex conjugate of 5 + 2i.
$= \frac{20i + 8(−1)}{25 + 10i − 10i − 4(−1)}$ $= \frac{20i − 8}{25 + 10i − 10i + 4}$	Simplify the result using the identity $i^2 = −1$.
$\mathbf{= \frac{20i − 8}{29}}$	Combine like terms.
$\mathbf{= \frac{−8}{29} + \frac{20}{29}i}$	Write the answer in the form $a + bi$.

Scientific Notation

SCIENTIFIC NOTATION is a method of representing very large and small numbers in the form $a \times 10^n$, where a is a value between 1 and 10, and n is a nonzero integer. For example, the number 927,000,000 is written in scientific notation as 9.27×10^8. Multiplying 9.27 by 10 eight

Figure 1.2. Scientific Notation

times gives 927,000,000. When performing operations with scientific notation, the final answer should be in the form $a \times 10^n$.

When adding and subtracting numbers in scientific notation, the power of 10 must be the same for all numbers. This results in like terms in which the a terms are added or subtracted and the 10^n remains unchanged. When multiplying numbers in scientific notation, multiply the a factors, and then multiply that answer by 10 to the sum of the exponents. For division, divide the a factors and subtract the exponents.

When multiplying numbers in scientific notation, add the exponents. When dividing, subtract the exponents.

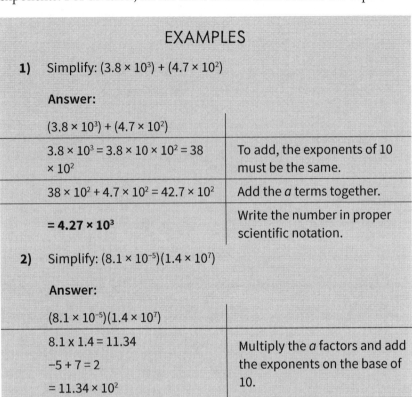

EXAMPLES

1) Simplify: $(3.8 \times 10^3) + (4.7 \times 10^2)$

Answer:

$(3.8 \times 10^3) + (4.7 \times 10^2)$	
$3.8 \times 10^3 = 3.8 \times 10 \times 10^2 = 38 \times 10^2$	To add, the exponents of 10 must be the same.
$38 \times 10^2 + 4.7 \times 10^2 = 42.7 \times 10^2$	Add the a terms together.
$= \mathbf{4.27 \times 10^3}$	Write the number in proper scientific notation.

2) Simplify: $(8.1 \times 10^{-5})(1.4 \times 10^7)$

Answer:

$(8.1 \times 10^{-5})(1.4 \times 10^7)$	
$8.1 \times 1.4 = 11.34$ $-5 + 7 = 2$ $= 11.34 \times 10^2$	Multiply the a factors and add the exponents on the base of 10.
$= \mathbf{1.134 \times 10^3}$	Write the number in proper scientific notation.

Positive and Negative Numbers

POSITIVE NUMBERS are greater than 0, and **NEGATIVE NUMBERS** are less than 0. Both positive and negative numbers can be shown on a **NUMBER LINE**.

-10 -9 -8 -7 -6 -5 -4 -3 -2 -1 0 1 2 3 4 5 6 7 8 9 10

Figure 1.3. Number Line

The **ABSOLUTE VALUE** of a number is the distance the number is from 0. Since distance is always positive, the absolute value of a number is always positive. The absolute value of a is denoted $|a|$. For example, $|-2| = 2$ since -2 is two units away from 0.

Positive and negative numbers can be added, subtracted, multiplied, and divided. The sign of the resulting number is governed by a specific set of rules shown in the table below.

Table 1.1. Operations with Positive and Negative Numbers

ADDING REAL NUMBERS		SUBTRACTING REAL NUMBERS*	
Positive + Positive = Positive	$7 + 8 = 15$	Negative – Positive = Negative	$-7 - 8 =$ $-7 + (-8) =$ -15
Negative + Negative = Negative	$-7 + (-8) =$ -15	Positive – Negative = Positive	$7 - (-8) =$ $7 + 8 = 15$
Negative + Positive OR Positive + Negative = Keep the sign of the number with larger absolute value	$-7 + 8 = 1$ $7 + -8 = -1$	Negative – Negative = Keep the sign of the number with larger absolute value	$-7 - (-8) =$ $-7 + 8 = 1$ $-8 - (-7) =$ $-8 + 7 = -1$

MULTIPLYING REAL NUMBERS		DIVIDING REAL NUMBERS	
Positive × Positive = Positive	$8 \times 4 = 32$	Positive ÷ Positive = Positive	$8 \div 4 = 2$
Negative × Negative = Positive	$-8 \times (-4)$ $= 32$	Negative ÷ Negative = Positive	$-8 \div (-4)$ $= 2$
Positive × Negative OR Negative × Positive = Negative	$8 \times (-4) =$ -32 $-8 \times 4 =$ -32	Positive ÷ Negative OR Negative ÷ Positive = Negative	$8 \div (-4)$ $= -2$ $-8 \div 4 = -2$

*Always change the subtraction to addition and change the sign of the second number; then use addition rules.

EXAMPLES

1) Add or subtract the following real numbers:

   A. $-18 + 12$

   B. $-3.64 + (-2.18)$

   C. $9.37 - 4.25$

   D. $86 - (-20)$

Answers:

A. Since $|-18| > |12|$, the answer is negative: $|-18| - |12| = 6$. So the answer is **–6**.

B. Adding two negative numbers results in a negative number. Add the values: **–5.82**.

C. The first number is larger than the second, so the final answer is positive: **5.12**.

D. Change the subtraction to addition, change the sign of the second number, and then add: $86 - (-20) = 86 + (+20) =$ **106**.

2) Multiply or divide the following real numbers:

A. $\left(\frac{10}{3}\right)\left(-\frac{9}{5}\right)$

B. $\frac{-64}{-10}$

C. $(2.2)(3.3)$

D. $-52 \div 13$

Answers:

A. Multiply the numerators, multiply the denominators, and simplify: $\frac{-90}{15} =$ **−6**.

B. A negative divided by a negative is a positive number: **6.4**.

C. Multiplying positive numbers gives a positive answer: **7.26**.

D. Dividing a negative by a positive number gives a negative answer: **−4**.

Order of Operations

The **order of operations** is simply the order in which operations are performed. **PEMDAS** is a common way to remember the order of operations:

1. **P**arentheses
2. **E**xponents
3. **M**ultiplication
4. **D**ivision
5. **A**ddition
6. **S**ubtraction

Multiplication and division, and addition and subtraction, are performed together from left to right. So, performing multiple operations on a set of numbers is a four-step process:

1. P: Calculate expressions inside parentheses, brackets, braces, etc.
2. E: Calculate exponents and square roots.
3. MD: Calculate any remaining multiplication and division in order from left to right.
4. AS: Calculate any remaining addition and subtraction in order from left to right.

Always work from left to right within each step when simplifying expressions.

EXAMPLES

1) Simplify: $2(21 - 14) + 6 \div (-2) \times 3 - 10$

Answer:

$2(21 - 14) + 6 \div (-2) \times 3 - 10$

$= 2(7) + 6 \div (-2) \times 3 - 10$	Calculate expressions inside parentheses.
$= 14 + 6 \div (-2) \times 3 - 10$ $= 14 + (-3) \times 3 - 10$ $= 14 + (-9) - 10$	There are no exponents or radicals, so perform multiplication and division from left to right.
$= 5 - 10$ $= \mathbf{-5}$	Perform addition and subtraction from left to right.

2) Simplify: $-(3)^2 + 4(5) + (5 - 6)^2 - 8$

Answer:

$-(3)^2 + 4(5) + (5 - 6)^2 - 8$	
$= -(3)^2 + 4(5) + (-1)^2 - 8$	Calculate expressions inside parentheses.
$= -9 + 4(5) + 1 - 8$	Simplify exponents and radicals.
$= -9 + 20 + 1 - 8$	Perform multiplication and division from left to right.
$= 11 + 1 - 8$ $= 12 - 8$ $= \mathbf{4}$	Perform addition and subtraction from left to right.

3) Simplify: $\dfrac{(7 - 9)^3 + 8(10 - 12)}{4^2 - 5^2}$

Answer:

$\dfrac{(7 - 9)^3 + 8(10 - 12)}{4^2 - 5^2}$	
$= \dfrac{(-2)^3 + 8(-2)}{4^2 - 5^2}$	Calculate expressions inside parentheses.
$= \dfrac{-8 + (-16)}{16 - 25}$	Simplify exponents and radicals.
$= \dfrac{-24}{-9}$	Perform addition and subtraction from left to right.
$= \dfrac{\mathbf{8}}{\mathbf{3}}$	Simplify.

Units of Measurement

The standard units for the metric and American systems are shown below, along with the prefixes used to express metric units.

GO ON

Table 1.2. Units and Conversion Factors

Dimension	American	SI
length	inch/foot/yard/mile	meter
mass	ounce/pound/ton	gram
volume	cup/pint/quart/gallon	liter
force	pound-force	newton
pressure	pound-force per square inch	pascal
work and energy	cal/British thermal unit	joule
temperature	Fahrenheit	kelvin
charge	faraday	coulomb

Table 1.3. Metric Prefixes

Prefix	Symbol	Multiplication Factor
tera	T	1,000,000,000,000
giga	G	1,000,000,000
mega	M	1,000,000
kilo	k	1,000
hecto	h	100
deca	da	10
base unit	--	--
deci	d	0.1
centi	c	0.01
milli	m	0.001
micro	µ	0.0000001
nano	n	0.0000000001
pico	p	0.0000000000001

A mnemonic device to help remember the metric system is *King Henry Drinks Under Dark Chocolate Moon* (KHDUDCM).

Units can be converted within a single system or between systems. When converting from one unit to another unit, a conversion factor (a numeric multiplier used to convert a value with a unit to another unit) is used. The process of converting between units using a conversion factor is sometimes known as dimensional analysis.

Table 1.4. Conversion Factors

1 in. = 2.54 cm	1 lb. = 0.454 kg
1 yd. = 0.914 m	1 cal = 4.19 J
1 mi. = 1.61 km	$1°F = \frac{5}{9}(°F - 32°C)$
1 gal. = 3.785 L	$1 cm^3 = 1 mL$
1 oz. = 28.35 g	1 hr = 3600 s

EXAMPLES

1) Convert the following measurements in the metric system.

   A. 4.25 kilometers to meters

   B. 8 m² to mm²

Answers:

   A. $4.25 \text{ km} \left(\frac{1000 \text{ m}}{1 \text{ km}} \right) = \textbf{4250 m}$

   B. $\frac{8 \text{ m}^2}{1} \times \frac{1000 \text{ mm}}{1 \text{ m}} \times \frac{1000 \text{ mm}}{1 \text{ m}} = \textbf{8,000,000 mm}^2$

Since the units are square units (m²), multiply by the conversion factor twice, so that both meters cancel.

2) Convert the following measurements in the American system.

   A. 12 feet to inches

   B. 7 yd² to ft²

Answers:

   A. $12 \text{ ft} \left(\frac{12 \text{ in}}{1 \text{ ft}} \right) = \textbf{144 in}$

   B. $7 \text{ yd}^2 \left(\frac{3\text{ft}^2}{1\text{yd}^2} \right) \left(\frac{3\text{ft}^2}{1\text{yd}^2} \right) = \textbf{63 ft}^2$

Since the units are square units (ft²), multiply by the conversion factor twice.

3) Convert the following measurements in the metric system to the American system.

   A. 23 meters to feet

   B. 10 m² to yd²

Answers:

   A. $23 \text{ m} \left(\frac{3.28 \text{ ft}}{1 \text{ m}} \right) = \textbf{75.44 ft}$

   B. $\frac{10 \text{ m}^2}{1} \times \frac{1.094 \text{ yd}}{1 \text{ m}} \times \frac{1.094 \text{ yd}}{1 \text{ m}} = \textbf{11.97 yd}^2$

4) Convert the following measurements in the American system to the metric system.

   A. 8 in³ to milliliters

   B. 16 kilograms to pounds

Answers:

   A. $8 \text{ in}^3 \left(\frac{16.39 \text{ ml}}{1 \text{ in}^3} \right) = \textbf{131.12 mL}$

   B. $16 \text{ kg} \left(\frac{2.2 \text{ lb}}{1 \text{ kg}} \right) = \textbf{35.2 lb}$

GO ON

Decimals and Fractions

Decimals

A DECIMAL is a number that contains a decimal point. A decimal number is an alternative way of writing a fraction. The place value for a decimal includes TENTHS (one place after the decimal), HUNDREDTHS (two places after the decimal), THOUSANDTHS (three places after the decimal), etc.

Table 1.5. Place Values

1,000,000	10^6	millions
100,000	10^5	hundred thousands
10,000	10^4	ten thousands
1,000	10^3	thousands
100	10^2	hundreds
10	10^1	tens
1	10^0	ones
.		decimal
$\frac{1}{10}$	10^{-1}	tenths
$\frac{1}{100}$	10^{-2}	hundredths
$\frac{1}{1000}$	10^{-3}	thousandths

Decimals can be added, subtracted, multiplied, and divided:

- To add or subtract decimals, line up the decimal point and perform the operation, keeping the decimal point in the same place in the answer.
- To multiply decimals, first multiply the numbers without the decimal points. Then, sum the number of decimal places to the right of the decimal point in the original numbers and place the decimal point in the answer so that there are that many places to the right of the decimal.
- When dividing decimals move the decimal point to the right in order to make the divisor a whole number and move the decimal the same number of places in the dividend. Divide the numbers without regard to the decimal. Then, place the decimal point of the quotient directly above the decimal point of the dividend.

To determine which way to move the decimal after multiplying, remember that changing the decimal should always make the final answer smaller.

$$4.2 \leftarrow \text{quotient}$$
$$2.5\overline{)10.5} \leftarrow \text{dividend}$$
$$\uparrow$$
divisor

Figure 1.4. Division Terms

EXAMPLES

1) Simplify: 24.38 + 16.51 − 29.87

Answer:

24.38 + 16.51 − 29.87	
24.38 + 16.51 = 40.89	Align the decimals and apply the order of operations left to right.
40.89 − 29.87 = **11.02**	

2) Simplify: (10.4)(18.2)

Answer:

(10.4)(18.2)	
104 × 182 = 18,928	Multiply the numbers ignoring the decimals.
18,928 → 189.28	The original problem includes two decimal places (one in each number), so move the decimal point in the answer so that there are two places after the decimal point.

Estimating is a good way to check the answer: 10.4 ≈ 10, 18.2 ≈ 18, and 10 × 18 = 180.

3) Simplify: 80 ÷ 2.5

Answer:

80 ÷ 2.5	
80 → 800 2.5 → 25	Move both decimals one place to the right (multiply by 10) so that the divisor is a whole number.
800 ÷ 25 = 32	Divide normally.

Fractions

A FRACTION is a number that can be written in the form $\frac{a}{b}$, where b is not equal to 0. The a part of the fraction is the NUMERATOR (top number) and the b part of the fraction is the DENOMINATOR (bottom number).

If the denominator of a fraction is greater than the numerator, the value of the fraction is less than 1 and it is called a PROPER FRACTION (for example, $\frac{3}{5}$ is a proper fraction). In an IMPROPER FRACTION, the denominator is less than the numerator and the value of the fraction is greater than 1 ($\frac{8}{3}$ is an improper fraction). An improper fraction can be written as a MIXED NUMBER, which has a whole number part and a proper fraction part. Improper fractions can be converted to mixed numbers by dividing the numerator by the denominator, which gives the whole number part, and the remainder becomes the numerator of the proper fraction part. (For example, the improper fraction $\frac{25}{9}$ is equal to mixed number $2\frac{7}{9}$ because 9 divides into 25 two times, with a remainder of 7.)

Conversely, mixed numbers can be converted to improper fractions. To do so, determine the numerator of the improper fraction by multiplying the denominator by the whole number, and then adding the numerator. The final number is written as the (now larger) numerator over the original denominator.

Fractions with the same denominator can be added or subtracted by simply adding or subtracting the numerators; the denominator will remain unchanged. To add or subtract fractions with different denominators, find the LEAST COMMON DENOMINATOR (LCD) of all the fractions. The LCD is the smallest number exactly divisible by each denominator. (For example, the least common denominator of the numbers 2, 3, and 8 is 24.) Once the LCD has been found, each fraction should be written in an equivalent form with the LCD as the denominator.

To multiply fractions, the numerators are multiplied together and denominators are multiplied together. If there are any mixed numbers, they should first be changed to improper fractions. Then, the numerators are multiplied together and the denominators are multiplied together. The fraction can then be reduced if necessary. To divide fractions, multiply the first fraction by the reciprocal of the second.

Any common denominator can be used to add or subtract fractions. The quickest way to find a common denominator of a set of values is simply to multiply all the values together. The result might not be the least common denominator, but it will allow the problem to be worked.

To convert mixed numbers to improper fractions:
$$a\frac{m}{n} = \frac{n \times a + m}{n}$$

$$\frac{a}{b} \pm \frac{c}{b} = \frac{a \pm c}{b}$$
$$\frac{a}{b} \times \frac{c}{d} = \frac{ac}{bd}$$
$$\frac{a}{b} \div \frac{c}{d} = \left(\frac{a}{b}\right)\left(\frac{d}{c}\right) = \frac{ad}{bc}$$

EXAMPLES

1) Simplify: $2\frac{3}{5} + 3\frac{1}{4} - 1\frac{1}{2}$

    Answer:

$2\frac{3}{5} + 3\frac{1}{4} - 1\frac{1}{2}$	
$= 2\frac{12}{20} + 3\frac{5}{20} - 1\frac{10}{20}$	Change each fraction so it has a denominator of 20, which is the LCD of 5, 4, and 2.
$2 + 3 - 1 = 4$ $\frac{12}{20} + \frac{5}{20} - \frac{10}{20} = \frac{7}{20}$	Add and subtract the whole numbers together and the fractions together.
$4\frac{7}{20}$	Combine to get the final answer (a mixed number).

2) Simplify: $\frac{7}{8} \times 3\frac{1}{3}$

Answer:

$\frac{7}{8} \times 3\frac{1}{3}$	
$3\frac{1}{3} = \frac{10}{3}$	Change the mixed number to an improper fraction.
$\frac{7}{8}\left(\frac{10}{3}\right) = \frac{7 \times 10}{8 \times 3}$ $= \frac{70}{24}$	Multiply the numerators together and the denominators together.
$= \frac{35}{12}$ $= 2\frac{11}{12}$	Reduce the fraction.

3) Simplify: $4\frac{1}{2} \div \frac{2}{3}$

Answer:

$4\frac{1}{2} \div \frac{2}{3}$	
$4\frac{1}{2} = \frac{9}{2}$	Change the mixed number to an improper fraction.
$\frac{9}{2} \div \frac{2}{3}$ $= \frac{9}{2} \times \frac{3}{2}$ $= \frac{27}{4}$	Multiply the first fraction by the reciprocal of the second fraction.
$= 6\frac{3}{4}$	Simplify.

Converting Between Fractions and Decimals

A fraction is converted to a decimal by using long division until there is no remainder and no pattern of repeating numbers occurs.

A decimal is converted to a fraction using the following steps:

- ◆ Place the decimal value as the numerator in a fraction with a denominator of 1.
- ◆ Multiply the fraction by $\frac{10}{10}$ for every digit in the decimal value, so that there is no longer a decimal in the numerator.
- ◆ Reduce the fraction.

EXAMPLES

1) Write the fraction $\frac{7}{8}$ as a decimal.

GO ON

Answer:

Divide the denominator into the numerator using long division.

$$\begin{array}{r} 0.875 \\ 8\overline{)7000} \\ -64 \\ \overline{60} \\ -56 \\ \overline{40} \end{array}$$

2) Write the fraction $\frac{5}{11}$ as a decimal.

Answer:

$$\begin{array}{r} 0.\overline{4545} \\ 11\overline{)50000} \\ -44 \\ \overline{60} \\ -55 \\ \overline{50} \\ -44 \\ \overline{60} \end{array}$$

Dividing using long division yields a repeating decimal.

3) Write the decimal 0.125 as a fraction.

Answer:

0.125	
$= \frac{0.125}{1}$	Create a fraction with 0.125 as the numerator and 1 as the denominator.
$\frac{0.125}{1} \times \frac{10}{10} \times \frac{10}{10} \times \frac{10}{10} = \frac{125}{1000}$	Multiple by $\frac{10}{10}$ three times (one for each numeral after the decimal).
$= \frac{1}{8}$	Simplify.

Alternatively, recognize that 0.125 is read "one hundred twenty-five thousandths" and can therefore be written in fraction form as $\frac{125}{1000}$.

Rounding and Estimation

ROUNDING is a way of simplifying a complicated number. The result of rounding will be a less precise value with which it is easier to write or perform operations. Rounding is performed to a specific place value, for example the thousands or tenths place.

The rules for rounding are as follows:

1. Underline the place value being rounded to.
2. Locate the digit one place value to the right of the underlined value. If this value is less than 5, then keep the underlined value and replace all digits to the right of the underlined value with 0. If the value to the right of the underlined digit

Estimation can often be used to eliminate answer choices on multiple-choice tests without having to work the problem to completion.

is greater than or equal to 5, then increase the underlined digit by one and replace all digits to the right of it with 0.

ESTIMATION is when numbers are rounded and then an operation is performed. This process can be used when working with large numbers to find a close, but not exact, answer.

EXAMPLES

1) Round the number 138,472 to the nearest thousands.

Answer:

$138,472 \approx \mathbf{138,000}$	The 8 is in the thousands place, and the number to its right is 4. Because 4 is less than 5, the 8 remains and all numbers to the right become 0.

2) The populations of five local towns are 12,341, 8975, 9431, 10,521, and 11,427. Estimate the total population to the nearest 1000 people.

Answer:

$12,341 \approx 12,000$	
$8975 \approx 9000$	
$9431 \approx 9000$	Round each value to the thousands place.
$10,521 \approx 11,000$	
$11,427 \approx 11,000$	
$12,000 + 9000 + 9000 + 11,000 + 11,000 = \mathbf{52,000}$	Add.

Ratios

A RATIO is a comparison of two numbers and can be represented as $\frac{a}{b}$, $a:b$, or a to b. The two numbers represent a constant relationship, not a specific value: for every a number of items in the first group, there will be b number of items in the second. For example, if the ratio of blue to red candies in a bag is 3:5, the bag will contain 3 blue candies for every 5 red candies. So, the bag might contain 3 blue candies and 5 red candies, or it might contain 30 blue candies and 50 red candies, or 36 blue candies and 60 red candies. All of these values are representative of the ratio 3:5 (which is the ratio in its lowest, or simplest, terms).

To find the "whole" when working with ratios, simply add the values in the ratio. For example, if the ratio of boys to girls in a class is 2:3, the "whole" is five: 2 out of every 5 students are boys, and 3 out of every 5 students are girls.

EXAMPLES

1) There are 10 boys and 12 girls in a first-grade class. What is the ratio of boys to the total number of students? What is the ratio of girls to boys?

Answer:

number of boys: 10 number of girls: 12 number of students: 22	Identify the variables.
number of boys : number of students $= 10 : 22$ $= \frac{10}{22}$ $= \frac{5}{11}$	Write out and simplify the ratio of boys to total students.
number of girls : number of boys $= 12 : 10$ $= \frac{12}{10}$ $= \frac{6}{5}$	Write out and simplify the ratio of girls to boys.

2) A family spends $600 a month on rent, $400 on utilities, $750 on groceries, and $550 on miscellaneous expenses. What is the ratio of the family's rent to their total expenses?

Answer:

rent $= 600$ utilities $= 400$ groceries $= 750$ miscellaneous $= 550$ total expenses $= 600 + 400 + 750 + 550 = 2300$	Identify the variables.
rent : total expenses $= 600 : 2300$ $= \frac{600}{2300}$ $= \frac{6}{23}$	Write out and simplify the ratio of rent to total expenses.

Proportions

A **PROPORTION** is an equation which states that two ratios are equal. A proportion is given in the form $\frac{a}{b} = \frac{c}{d}$, where the a and d terms are the extremes and the b and c terms are the means. A proportion is solved using cross-multiplication ($ad = bc$) to create an equation with no fractional components. A proportion must have the same units in both numerators and both denominators.

EXAMPLES

1) Solve the proportion for x: $\frac{3x-5}{2}=\frac{x-8}{3}$.

Answer:

$\frac{(3x-5)}{2}=\frac{(x-8)}{3}$	
$3(3x-5)=2(x-8)$	Cross-multiply.
$9x-15=2x-16$	
$7x-15=-16$	
$7x=-1$	Solve the equation for x.
$x=-\frac{1}{7}$	

2) A map is drawn such that 2.5 inches on the map equates to an actual distance of 40 miles. If the distance measured on the map between two cities is 17.25 inches, what is the actual distance between them in miles?

Answer:

$\frac{2.5}{40}=\frac{17.25}{x}$	Write a proportion where x equals the actual distance and each ratio is written as inches : miles.
$2.5x=690$	
$x=276$	Cross-multiply and divide to solve for x.
The two cities are **276 miles apart**.	

3) A factory knows that 4 out of 1000 parts made will be defective. If in a month there are 125,000 parts made, how many of these parts will be defective?

Answer:

$\frac{4}{1000}=\frac{x}{125,000}$	Write a proportion where x is the number of defective parts made and both ratios are written as defective : total.
$1000x=500,000$	
$x=500$	Cross-multiply and divide to solve for x.
There are **500 defective parts** for the month.	

Percentages

A PERCENT (or percentage) means per hundred and is expressed with a percent symbol (%). For example, 54% means 54 out of every 100. A percent can be converted to a decimal by removing the % symbol and moving the decimal point two places to the left, while a decimal can be converted to a percent by moving the decimal point two places to the right and attaching the % sign. A percent can be converted to a fraction by writing the percent as a fraction with 100 as the denominator and reducing. A fraction can be converted to a percent by performing the indicated division, multiplying the result by 100, and attaching the % sign.

The equation for finding percentages has three variables: the part, the whole, and the percent (which is expressed in the equation as a decimal). The equation, as shown below, can be rearranged to solve for any of these variables.

- part = whole × percent
- percent = $\frac{\text{part}}{\text{whole}}$
- whole = $\frac{\text{part}}{\text{percent}}$

This set of equations can be used to solve percent word problems. All that's needed is to identify the part, whole, and/or percent, and then to plug those values into the appropriate equation and solve.

EXAMPLES

1) Change the following values to the indicated form:

   A. 18% to a fraction

   B. $\frac{3}{5}$ to a percent

   C. 1.125 to a percent

   D. 84% to a decimal

   Answers:

   A. The percent is written as a fraction over 100 and reduced: $\frac{18}{100} = \frac{9}{50}$.

   B. Dividing 5 by 3 gives the value 0.6, which is then multiplied by 100: **60%**.

   C. The decimal point is moved two places to the right: $1.125 \times 100 = \textbf{112.5\%}$.

   D. The decimal point is moved two places to the left: $84 \div 100 = \textbf{0.84}$.

2) In a school of 650 students, 54% of the students are boys. How many students are girls?

Answer:

Percent of students who are girls = 100% − 54% = 46% percent = 46% = 0.46 whole = 650 students part = ?	Identify the variables.
part = whole × percent = 0.46 × 650 = 299 **There are 299 girls.**	Plug the variables into the appropriate equation.

Percent Change

Percent change problems involve a change from an original amount. Often percent change problems appear as word problems that include discounts, growth, or markups. In order to solve percent change problems, it's necessary to identify the percent change (as a decimal), the amount of change, and the original amount. (Keep in mind that one of these will be the value being solved for.) These values can then be plugged into the equations below:

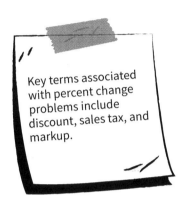

Key terms associated with percent change problems include discount, sales tax, and markup.

- amount of change = original amount × percent change
- percent change = $\dfrac{\text{amount of change}}{\text{original amount}}$
- original amount = $\dfrac{\text{amount of change}}{\text{percent change}}$

EXAMPLES

1) An HDTV that originally cost $1,500 is on sale for 45% off. What is the sale price for the item?

Answer:

original amount =$1,500 percent change = 45% = 0.45 amount of change = ?	Identify the variables.
amount of change = original amount × percent change = 1500 × 0.45 = 675	Plug the variables into the appropriate equation.
1500 − 675 = 825 **The final price is $825.**	To find the new price, subtract the amount of change from the original price.

2) A house was bought in 2000 for $100,000 and sold in 2015 for $120,000. What was the percent growth in the value of the house from 2000 to 2015?

Answer:

original amount = \$100,000 amount of change = 120,000 − 100,000 = 20,000 percent change = ?	Identify the variables.
percent change = $\dfrac{\text{amount of change}}{\text{original amount}}$ $= \dfrac{20,000}{100,000}$ $= 0.20$	Plug the variables into the appropriate equation.
$0.20 \times 100 = \textbf{20\%}$	To find the percent growth, multiply by 100.

Comparison of Rational Numbers

Rational numbers can be ordered from least to greatest (or greatest to least) by placing them in the order in which they fall on a number line. When comparing a set of fractions, it's often easiest to convert each value to a common denominator. Then, it's only necessary to compare the numerators of each fraction.

When working with numbers in multiple forms (for example, a group of fractions and decimals), convert the values so that the set contains only fractions or only decimals. When ordering negative numbers, remember that the negative numbers with the largest absolute values are farthest from 0 and are therefore the smallest numbers. (For example, –75 is smaller than –25.)

Drawing a number line can help when comparing numbers: the final list should go in order from left to right (least to greatest) or right to left (greatest to least) on the line.

EXAMPLES

1) Order the following numbers from greatest to least: $-\frac{2}{3}$, 1.2, 0, $-2.1, \frac{5}{4}, 1, \frac{1}{8}$.

Answer:

$-\frac{2}{3} = -0.\overline{66}$ $\frac{5}{4} = 1.25$ $\frac{1}{8} = 0.125$	Change each fraction to a decimal.
$1.25, 1.2, 0.125, 0, -0.\overline{66}, -1,$ -2.1	Place the decimals in order from greatest to least.
$\frac{5}{4}, 1.2, \frac{1}{8}, 0, -\frac{2}{3}, -1, -2.1$	Convert back to fractions if the problem requires it.

2) Order the following numbers from least to greatest: $\frac{1}{3}, -\frac{5}{6}, 1\frac{1}{8},$ $\frac{7}{12}, -\frac{3}{4}, -\frac{3}{2}.$

Answer:

$\frac{1}{3} = \frac{8}{24}$ $-\frac{5}{6} = -\frac{20}{24}$ $1\frac{1}{8} = \frac{9}{8} = \frac{27}{24}$ $\frac{7}{12} = \frac{14}{24}$ $-\frac{3}{4} = -\frac{18}{24}$ $-\frac{3}{2} = -\frac{36}{24}$	Convert each value using the least common denominator of 24.
$-\frac{36}{24}, -\frac{20}{24}, -\frac{18}{24}, \frac{8}{24}, \frac{14}{24}, \frac{27}{24}$	Arrange the fractions in order from least to greatest by comparing the numerators.
$-\frac{3}{2}, -\frac{5}{6}, -\frac{3}{4}, \frac{1}{3}, \frac{7}{12}, 1\frac{1}{8}$	Put the fractions back in their original form if the problem requires it.

Exponents and Radicals

Exponents

An expression in the form b^n is in an exponential notation where b is the BASE and n is an EXPONENT. To perform the operation, multiply the base by itself the number of times indicated by the exponent. For example, 2^3 is equal to $2 \times 2 \times 2$ or 8.

Table 1.6. Operations with Exponents

RULE	EXAMPLE	EXPLANATION
$a^0 = 1$	$5^0 = 1$	Any base (except 0) to the 0 power is 1.
$a^n = \frac{1}{a^n}$	$5^3 = \frac{1}{5^3}$	A negative exponent becomes positive when moved from numerator to denominator (or vice versa).
$a^m a^n = a^{m+n}$	$5^3 5^4 = 5^{3+4} = 5^7$	Add the exponents to multiply two powers with the same base.
$(a^m)^n$	$(5^3)^4 = 5^{3(4)} = 5^{12}$	Multiply the exponents to raise a power to a power.
$\frac{a^m}{a^n} = a^{m-n}$	$\frac{5^4}{5^3} = 5^{4-3} = 5^1$	Subtract the exponents to divide two powers with the same base.
$(ab)^n = a^n b^n$	$(5 \times 6)^3 = 5^3 6^3$	Apply the exponent to each base to raise a product to a power.
$\frac{a}{b}^n = \frac{a^n}{b^n}$	$\frac{(5/6)^3}{6} = \frac{5^3}{6^3}$	Apply the exponent to each base to raise a quotient to a power.

Table 1.6. Operations with Exponents (continued)

RULE	EXAMPLE	EXPLANATION
$\dfrac{(a/b)^{-n}}{b} = \dfrac{b}{a}$	$\dfrac{(5/6)^{-3}}{6} = \dfrac{(6/5)^3}{5}$	Invert the fraction and change the sign of the exponent to raise a fraction to a negative power.
$\dfrac{a^m}{b^n} = \dfrac{(b/a)^n}{a^m}$	$\dfrac{5^3}{6^4} = \dfrac{6^4}{5^3}$	Change the sign of the exponent when moving a number from the numerator to denominator (or vice versa).

EXAMPLES

1) Simplify: $\dfrac{(10^2)^3}{(10^2)^2}$

Answer:

$\dfrac{(10^2)^3}{(10^2)^2}$	
$= \dfrac{10^6}{10^{-4}}$	Multiply the exponents raised to a power.
$= 10^{6-(-4)}$	Subtract the exponent in the denominator from the one in the numerator.
$= 10^{10}$ $= \mathbf{10,000,000,000}$	Simplify.

2) Simplify: $\dfrac{(x^{-2}y^2)^2}{x^3 y}$

Answer:

$\dfrac{(x^{-2}y^2)^2}{x^3 y}$	
$= \dfrac{x^{-4}y^4}{x^3 y}$	Multiply the exponents raised to a power.
$= x^{-4-3}y^{4-1}$ $= x^{-7}y^3$	Subtract the exponent in the denominator from the one in the numerator.
$= \dfrac{y^3}{x^7}$	Move negative exponents to the denominator.

Radicals

RADICALS are expressed as $\sqrt[b]{a}$, where b is called the INDEX and a is the RADICAND. A radical is used to indicate the inverse operation of an exponent: finding the base which can be raised to b to yield a. For example, $\sqrt[3]{125}$ is equal to 5 because $5 \times 5 \times 5$ equals 125. The same operation can be expressed using a fraction exponent, so $\sqrt[b]{a} = \dfrac{1}{a^b}$. Note that when no value is indicated for b, it is assumed to be 2 (square root).

24 Accepted, Inc. ¦ TASC Math Book Study Guide

When b is even and a is positive, $\sqrt[b]{a}$ is defined to be the positive real value n such that $n^b = a$ (example: $\sqrt{16} = 4$ only, and not -4, even though $(-4)(-4) = 16$). If b is even and a is negative, $\sqrt[b]{a}$ will be a complex number (example: $\sqrt{-9} = 3i$). Finally if b is odd, $\sqrt[b]{a}$ will always be a real number regardless of the sign of a. If a is negative, $\sqrt[b]{a}$ will be negative since a number to an odd power is negative (example: $\sqrt[5]{-32} = -2$ since $(-2)^5 = -32$).

$\sqrt[n]{x}$ is referred to as the nth root of x.

- ◆ $n = 2$ is the square root
- ◆ $n = 3$ is the cube root
- ◆ $n = 4$ is the fourth root
- ◆ $n = 5$ is the fifth root

The following table of operations with radicals holds for all cases EXCEPT the case where b is even and a is negative (the complex case).

Table 1.7. Operations with Radicals

RULE	EXAMPLE	EXPLANATION
$\sqrt[b]{ac} = \sqrt[b]{a}\,\sqrt[b]{c}$	$\sqrt[3]{81} = \sqrt[3]{27}\,\sqrt[3]{3} = 3\sqrt[3]{3}$	The values under the radical sign can be separated into values that multiply to the original value.
$\sqrt[b]{\dfrac{a}{c}} = \dfrac{\sqrt[b]{a}}{\sqrt[b]{c}}$	$\sqrt{\dfrac{4}{81}} = \dfrac{\sqrt{4}}{\sqrt{81}} = \dfrac{2}{9}$	The b-root of the numerator and denominator can be calculated when there is a fraction under a radical sign.
$\sqrt[b]{a^c} = (\sqrt[b]{a})^c = a^{\frac{c}{b}}$	$\sqrt[3]{6^2} = (\sqrt[3]{6})^2 = 6^{\frac{2}{3}}$	The b-root can be written as a fractional exponent. If there is a power under the radical sign, it will be the numerator of the fraction.
$\dfrac{c}{\sqrt[b]{a}} \times \dfrac{\sqrt[b]{a}}{\sqrt[b]{a}} = \dfrac{c\sqrt[b]{a}}{a}$	$\dfrac{5}{\sqrt{2}}\dfrac{\sqrt{2}}{\sqrt{2}} = \dfrac{5\sqrt{2}}{2}$	To rationalize the denominator, multiply the numerator and denominator by the radical in the denominator until the radical has been canceled out.
$\dfrac{c}{b - \sqrt{a}} \times \dfrac{b + \sqrt{a}}{b + \sqrt{a}}$ $= \dfrac{c(b + \sqrt{a})}{b^2 - a}$	$\dfrac{4}{3 - \sqrt{2}}\dfrac{3 + \sqrt{2}}{3 + \sqrt{2}}$ $= \dfrac{4(3 + \sqrt{2})}{9 - 2} = \dfrac{12 + 4\sqrt{2}}{7}$	To rationalize the denominator, the numerator and denominator are multiplied by the conjugate of the denominator.

EXAMPLES

1) Simplify: $\sqrt{48}$

Answer:

$\sqrt{48}$	
$= \sqrt{16 \times 3}$	Determine the largest square number that is a factor of the radicand (48) and write the radicand as a product using that square number as a factor.
$= \sqrt{16}\,\sqrt{3}$ $= \mathbf{4\sqrt{3}}$	Apply the rules of radicals to simplify.

2) Simplify: $\dfrac{6}{\sqrt{8}}$

Answer:

$\dfrac{6}{\sqrt{8}}$	
$= \dfrac{6}{\sqrt{4}\,\sqrt{2}}$ $= \dfrac{6}{2\sqrt{2}}$	Apply the rules of radicals to simplify.
$= \dfrac{6}{2\sqrt{2}}\left(\dfrac{\sqrt{2}}{\sqrt{2}}\right)$ $= \dfrac{\mathbf{3\sqrt{2}}}{\mathbf{2}}$	Multiply by $\dfrac{\sqrt{2}}{\sqrt{2}}$ to rationalize the denominator.

Factorials

A **FACTORIAL** of a number n is denoted by $n!$ and is equal to $1 \times 2 \times 3 \times 4 \times \dots \times n$. Both $0!$ and $1!$ are equal to 1 by definition. Fractions containing factorials can often be simplified by crossing out the portions of the factorials that occur in both the numerator and denominator.

EXAMPLES

1) Simplify: $8!$

Answer:

$8!$	
$= 8 \times 7 \times 6 \times 5 \times 4 \times 3 \times 2 \times 1$ $= \mathbf{40{,}320}$	Expand the factorial and multiply.

2) Simplify: $\dfrac{10!}{7!3!}$

Answer:

$\dfrac{10!}{7!3!}$	
$= \dfrac{10 \times 9 \times 8 \times 7!}{7! \times 3 \times 2 \times 1}$	Expand the factorial.

$= \dfrac{10 \times 9 \times 8}{3 \times 2 \times 1}$	Cross out values that occur in both the numerator and denominator.
$= \dfrac{720}{6}$ $= \mathbf{120}$	Multiply and simplify.

Sequences and Series

Sequences can be thought of as a set of numbers (called TERMS) with a rule that explains the particular pattern between the terms. The terms of a sequence are separated by commas. There are two types of sequences that will be examined, arithmetic and geometric. The sum of an arithmetic sequence is known as an ARITHMETIC SERIES; similarly the sum of a geometric sequence is known as a GEOMETRIC SERIES.

Arithmetic Sequences

ARITHMETIC GROWTH is constant growth, meaning that the difference between any one term in the series and the next consecutive term will be the same constant. This constant is called the COMMON DIFFERENCE. Thus, to list the terms in the sequence, one can just add (or subtract) the same number repeatedly. For example, the series {20, 30, 40, 50} is arithmetic since 10 is added each time to get from one term to the next. One way to represent this sequence is using a RECURSIVE definition, which basically says: *next term = current term + common difference*. For this example, the recursive definition would be $a_{n+1} = a_n + 10$ because the *next* term a_{n+1} in the sequence is the current term a_n plus 10. In general, the recursive definition of a series is:

$a_{n+1} = a_n + d$, where d is the common difference.

Often, the objective of arithmetic sequence questions is to find a specific term in the sequence or the sum of a certain series of terms. The formulas to use are:

Table 1.8. Formulas for Arithmetic Sequences and Series

FINDING THE NTH TERM . . .

$a_n = a_1 + d(n-1)$ $a_n = a_m + d(n - m)$	d = the common difference of the sequence a_n = the nth term in the sequence n = the number of the term a_m = the mth term in the sequence m = the number of the term a_1 = the first term in the sequence

Table 1.8. Formulas for Arithmetic Sequences and Series (continued)

FINDING THE PARTIAL SUM . . .

$S_n = \dfrac{n(a_1 + a_n)}{2}$	S_n = sum of the terms through the nth term
	a_n = the nth term in the sequence
	n = the number of the term
	a_1 = the first term in the sequence

EXAMPLES

1) Find the ninth term of the sequence: −57, −40, −23, −6 …

   Answer:

$a_1 = -57$ $d = -57 - (-40) = 17$ $n = 9$	Identify the variables given.
$a_9 = -57 + 17(9 - 1)$	Plug these values into the formula for the specific term of an arithmetic sequence.
$a_9 = -57 + 17(8)$ $a_9 = -57 + 136$ $\boldsymbol{a_9 = 79}$	Solve for a_9.

2) If the 23rd term in an arithmetic sequence is 820, and the 5th term is 200, find the common difference between each term.

   Answer:

$a_5 = 200$ $a_{23} = 820$ $n = 23$ $m = 5$ $d = ?$	Idenfity the variables given.
$a_n = a_m + d(n - m)$ $820 = 200 + d(23 - 5)$ $620 = d(18)$ $\boldsymbol{d = 34.\overline{44}}$	Plug these values into the equation for using one term to find another in an arithmetic sequence.

3) Evaluate $\sum_{n=14}^{45} 2n + 10$.

   Answer:

$a_1 = 2(1) + 10 = 12$ $n = 45$ $a_n = 2(45) + 10 = 100$	Find the partial sum of the first 45 terms.

$S_n = \dfrac{n(a_1 + a_n)}{2}$ $= \dfrac{45(12 + 100)}{2}$ $= 2520$	
$a_1 = 2(1) + 10 = 12$ $n = 13$ $a_n = 2(13) + 10 = 36$ $S_n = \dfrac{n(a_1 + a_n)}{2}$ $= \dfrac{13(12 + 36)}{2}$ $= 312$	Find the partial sum of the first 13 terms.
$S_{45} - S_{13} = 2520 - 312$ $= \mathbf{2208}$	The sum of the terms between 14 and 45 will be the difference between S_{45} and S_{13}.

Geometric Sequences

While an arithmetic sequence has an additive pattern, a GEOMETRIC SEQUENCE has a multiplicative pattern. This means that to get from any one term in the sequence to the next term in the sequence, the term is multiplied by a fixed number (called the COMMON RATIO). The following sequence is a geometric sequence: {8, 4, 2, 1, .5, .25, .125}. In this case, the multiplier (or common ratio) is $\frac{1}{2}$. The multiplier can be any real number other than 0 or 1. To find the common ratio, simply choose any term in the sequence and divide it by the previous term (this is the ratio of two consecutive terms—thus the name common *ratio*). In the above example, the ratio between the second and third terms is $\frac{2}{4} = \frac{1}{2}$.

Geometric sequences require their own formulas to find the next term and a sum of a specific series.

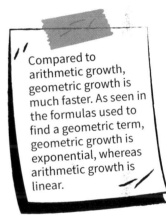

Compared to arithmetic growth, geometric growth is much faster. As seen in the formulas used to find a geometric term, geometric growth is exponential, whereas arithmetic growth is linear.

Table 1.9. Geometric Sequences: Formulas

FINDING THE *N*TH TERM . . .

$a_n = a_1 \times r^{n-1}$ $a_n = a_m \times r^{n-m}$	r = the common ratio of the sequence a_n = the nth term in the sequence n = the number of the term a_m = the mth term in the sequence m = the number of the term a_1 = the first term in the sequence

Table 1.9. Geometric Sequences: Formulas (continued)

FINDING THE PARTIAL SUM . . .

$$S_n = \frac{a_1(1 - r^n)}{1 - r}$$	S_n = sum of the terms through the nth term
	r = the common ratio of the sequence
	a_n = the nth term in the sequence
	n = the number of the term
	a_1 = the first term in the sequence

FINDING THE SUM OF AN INFINITE SERIES . . .

$$S_\infty = \frac{a}{1 - r}$$ $(|r| < 1)$	S_∞ = sum of all terms
	r = the common ratio of the sequence
	a = the fifth term in the sequence

The finite sum formula works similarly to the arithmetic sequence sum. However, sometimes the INFINITE SUM of the sequence must be found. The sum of an infinite number of terms of a sequence is called a SERIES. If the infinite terms of the sequence add up to a finite number, the series is said to CONVERGE to that number. If the sum of the terms is infinite, then the series DIVERGES. Another way to say this is to ask: is there a limit to the finite sum S_n as n goes to infinity? For geometric series in the form $\sum_{n=1}^{\infty} a \times r^n$, the series converges only when $|r| < 1$ (or $-1 < r < 1$). If r is greater than 1, the sum will approach infinity, so the series diverges.

EXAMPLES

1) Find the 8th term in the sequence: {13, 39, 117, 351 . . .}

   Answer:

$a_1 = 13$ $n = 8$ $r = \frac{39}{13} = 3$	Identify the variables given.
$a_8 = 13 \times 3^{8-1}$ $a_8 = 13 \times 2187 = 28{,}431$	Plug these values into the equation to find a specific term in a geometric sequence.
The eighth term of the given sequence is **28,431**.	

2) Find the sum of the first 10 terms of this sequence: {−4, 16, −64, 256 . . .}

Answer:

$a_1 = -4$ $n = 10$ $r = \dfrac{16}{-4} = -4$	Identify the variables given.
$\begin{aligned} S_{10} &= \frac{-4(1-(-4)^{10})}{1-(-4)} \\[4pt] &= \frac{-4(1-1{,}048{,}576)}{5} \\[4pt] &= \frac{4{,}194{,}300}{5} \\[4pt] &= \mathbf{838{,}860} \end{aligned}$	Plug these values into the equation for the partial sum of a geometric sequence.

Test Your Skills

1) To which of the following number sets does 3 not belong?

   A. irrational

   B. rational

   C. whole

   D. integer

2) Simplify: $\frac{3}{2-i}$

   A. $2 + i$

   B. $6 + 3i$

   C. $\frac{2+i}{5}$

   D. $\frac{6+3i}{5}$

3) Simplify: $(4.71 \times 10^3) - (2.98 \times 10^2)$

   A. 1.73×10

   B. 4.412×10^2

   C. 1.73×10^3

   D. 4.412×10^3

4) Simplify: $(1.2 \times 10^{-3})(1.13 \times 10^{-4})$

   A. 1.356×10^{-7}

   B. 1.356×10^{-1}

   C. 1.356×10

   D. 1.356×10^{12}

5) Simplify: $-(3^2) + (5 - 7)^2 - 3(4 - 8)$

   A. -17

   B. -1

   C. 7

   D. 25

6) Which of the following is listed in order from least to greatest?

   A. $-0.95, 0, \frac{2}{5}, 0.35, \frac{3}{4}$

   B. $-1, -\frac{1}{10}, -0.11, \frac{5}{6}, 0.75$

   C. $-\frac{3}{4}, -0.2, 0, \frac{2}{3}, 0.55$

   D. $-1.1, -\frac{4}{5}, -0.13, 0.7, \frac{9}{11}$

7) Simplify: $\frac{(3x^2y^2)^2}{3^3x^{-2}y^3}$

   A. $3x^6y$

   B. $\frac{x^6y}{3}$

   C. $\frac{x^4}{3y}$

   D. $\frac{3x^4}{y}$

8) Simplify: $\sqrt[3]{64} + \sqrt[3]{729}$

   A. 13

   B. 17

   C. 31

   D. 35

9) If a student answers 42 out of 48 questions correctly on a quiz, what percentage of questions did she answer correctly?

   Write in the answer: _____

10) If an employee who makes $37,500 per year receives a 5.5% raise, what is the employee's new salary?

   Write in the answer: _____

GO ON

Answer Key

1)   **A.** The number 3 is not irrational because it can be written as the fraction $\frac{3}{1}$.

2)   **D.** Multiply by the complex conjugate and simplify.

$\frac{3}{2-i}$

Multiply: $\left(\frac{3}{2-i}\right)\left(\frac{2+i}{2+i}\right)$

$\frac{3(2+i)}{4-2i+2i-i^2}$

$= \frac{3(2+i)}{4-(-1)}$

$= \frac{(6+3i)}{5}$

3)   **D.** Make the exponents the same and subtract the digit parts of each term.

$(4.71 \times 10^3) - (2.98 \times 10^2)$

$4.71 \times 10 \times 10^2 = 47.1 \times 10^2$

$47.1 - 2.98 = 44.12$

$44.12 \times 10^2 = \mathbf{4.412 \times 10^3}$

4)   **A.** Multiply the digits and add the exponents.

$(1.2 \times 10^{-3})(1.13 \times 10^{-4})$

$1.2 \times 1.13 = 1.356$

$-3 + (-4) = -7$

$\mathbf{1.356 \times 10^{-7}}$

5)   **C.** Simplify using PEMDAS.

$-(3^2) + (5-7)^2 - 3(4-8)$

$= -(3^2) + (-2)^2 - 3(-4)$

$= -9 + 4 - 3(-4)$

$= -9 + 4 + 12 = \mathbf{7}$

6)   **D.** Write each value in decimal form and compare.

$-0.95 < 0 < 0.4 < 0.35 < 0.75$ FALSE

$-1 < -0.1 < -0.11 < 0.8\overline{3} < 0.75$ FALSE

$-0.75 < -0.2 < 0 < 0.\overline{66} < 0.55$ FALSE

$-1.1 < -0.8 < -0.13 < 0.7 < 0.\overline{81}$ TRUE

7)   **B.** Use the rules of exponents to simplify the expression.

$\frac{(3x^2y^2)^2}{3^3x^{-2}y^3} = \frac{3^2x^4y^4}{3^3x^{-2}y^3} = \frac{x^6y}{3}$

8)   **A.** Simplify each root and add.

$\sqrt[3]{64} = 4$

$\sqrt[3]{729} = 9$

$4 + 9 = \mathbf{13}$

9)   Use the formula for percentages.

$percent = \frac{part}{whole}$

$= \frac{42}{48}$

$= 0.875 = \mathbf{87.5\%}$

10)   Find the amount of change and add to the original amount.

amount of change =
original amount × percent change

$= 37{,}500 \times 0.055 = 2{,}062.50$

$37{,}500 + 2{,}062.50 = \mathbf{\$39{,}562.50}$

two

ALGEBRA

lgebra, meaning "restoration" in Arabic, is the mathematical method of finding the unknown. The first algebraic book in Egypt was used to figure out complex inheritances that were to be split among many individuals. Today, algebra is just as necessary when dealing with unknown amounts.

Algebraic Expressions

The foundation of algebra is the **VARIABLE**, an unknown number represented by a symbol (usually a letter such as x or a). Variables can be preceded by a **COEFFICIENT**, which is a constant (i.e., a real number) in front of the variable, such as $4x$ or $-2a$. An **ALGEBRAIC EXPRESSION** is any sum, difference, product, or quotient of variables and numbers (for example $3x^2$, $2x + 7y - 1$, and $\frac{5}{x}$ are algebraic expressions). **TERMS** are any quantities that are added or subtracted (for example, the terms of the expression $x^2 - 3x + 5$ are x^2, $3x$, and 5). A **POLYNOMIAL EXPRESSION** is an algebraic expression where all the exponents on the variables are whole numbers. A polynomial with only two terms is known as a **BINOMIAL**, and one with three terms is a **TRINOMIAL**. A **MONOMIAL** has only one term.

Simplified expressions are ordered by variable terms alphabetically with highest exponent first then down to constants.

EVALUATING EXPRESSIONS is another way of saying "find the numeric value of an expression if the variable is equal to a certain number." To evaluate the expression, simply plug the given value(s) for the variable(s) into the equation and simplify. Remember to use the order of operations when simplifying:

1.	Parentheses	4.	Division
2.	Exponents	5.	Addition
3.	Multiplication	6.	Subtraction

EXAMPLE

If $m = 4$, find the value of the following expression:

$5(m - 2)^3 + 3m^2 - \frac{m}{4} - 1$

Answer:

$5(m - 2)^3 + 3m^2 - \frac{m}{4} - 1$	
$= 5(4 - 2)^3 + 3(4)^2 - \frac{4}{4} - 1$	Plug the value 4 in for m in the expression.
$= 5(2)^3 + 3(4)^2 - \frac{4}{4} - 1$	Calculate all the expressions inside the parentheses.
$= 5(8) + 3(16) - \frac{4}{4} - 1$	Simplify all exponents.
$= 40 + 48 - 1 - 1$	Perform multiplication and division from left to right.
$= 86$	Perform addition and subtraction from left to right.

Operations with Expressions

Adding and Subtracting

Expressions can be added or subtracted by simply adding and subtracting LIKE TERMS, which are terms with the same variable part (the variables must be the same, with the same exponents on each variable). For example, in the expressions $2x + 3xy - 2z$ and $6y + 2xy$, the like terms are $3xy$ and $2xy$. Adding the two expressions yields the new expression $2x + 6xy - 2z + 6y$. Note that the other terms did not change; they cannot be combined because they have different variables.

EXAMPLE

If $a = 12x + 7xy - 9y$ and $b = 8x - 9xz + 7z$, what is $a + b$?

Answer:

$a + b =$ $(12x + 8x) + 7xy - 9y - 9xz$ $+ 7z =$ $\mathbf{20x + 7xy - 9y - 9xz + 7z}$	The only like terms in both expressions are 12x and 8x, so these two terms will be added, and all other terms will remain the same.

Operations with polynomials can always be checked by evaluating equivalent expressions for the same value.

Distributing and Factoring

Distributing and factoring can be seen as two sides of the same coin. DISTRIBUTION multiplies each term in the first factor by each term in the second factor to get rid of parentheses. FACTORING reverses this process, taking a polynomial in standard form and writing it as a product of two or more factors.

When distributing a monomial through a polynomial, the expression outside the parentheses is multiplied by each term inside the parentheses. Using the rules of exponents, coefficients are multiplied and exponents are added.

When simplifying two polynomials, each term in the first polynomial must multiply each term in the second polynomial. A binomial (two terms) multiplied by a binomial, will require 2 × 2 or 4 multiplications. For the binomial × binomial case, this process is sometimes called **FOIL**, which stands for first, outside, inside, and last. These terms refer to the placement of each term of the expression: multiply the first term in each expression, then the outside terms, then the inside terms, and finally the last terms. A binomial (two terms) multiplied by a trinomial (three terms), will require 2 × 3 or 6 products to simplify. The first term in the first polynomial multiplies each of the three terms in the second polynomial, then the second term in the first polynomial multiplies each of the three terms in the second polynomial. A trinomial (three terms) by a trinomial will require 3 × 3 or 9 products, and so on.

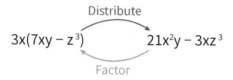

Figure 2.1. Distribution and Factoring

Factoring is the reverse of distributing: the first step is always to remove ("undistribute") the GCF of all the terms, if there is a GCF (besides 1). The GCF is the product of any constants and/or variables that <u>every</u> term shares. (For example, the GCF of $12x^3$, $15x^2$ and $6xy^2$ is $3x$ because $3x$ evenly divides all three terms.) This shared factor can be taken out of each term and moved to the outside of the parentheses, leaving behind a polynomial where each term is the original term divided by the GCF. (The remaining terms for the terms in the example would be $4x^2$, $5x$, and $2xy$.) It may be possible to factor the polynomial in the parentheses further, depending on the problem.

EXAMPLES

1) Expand the following expression: $5x(x^2 - 2c + 10)$

Answer:

$5x(x^2 - 2c + 10)$

$(5x)(x^2) = 5x^3$

$(5x)(-2c) = -10xc$

$(5x)(10) = 50x$

Distribute and multiply the term outside the parentheses to all three terms inside the parentheses.

$= \mathbf{5x^3 - 10xc + 50x}$

2) Expand the following expression: $(x^2 - 5)(2x - x^3)$

Answer:

$(x^2 - 5)(2x - x^3)$	
$(x^2)(2x) = 2x^3$ $(x^2)(-x^3) = -x^5$ $(-5)(2x) = -10x$ $(-5)(-x^3) = 5x^3$	Apply FOIL: first, outside, inside, and last.
$= 2x^3 - x^5 - 10x + 5x^3$	Combine like terms and put them in order.
$= -x^5 + 7x^3 - 10x$	

3) Factor the expression $16z^2 + 48z$

Answer:

$16z^2 + 48z$ $= 16z(z + 3)$	Both terms have a z, and 16 is a common factor of both 16 and 48. So the greatest common factor is $16z$. Factor out the GCF.

4) Factor the expression $6m^3 + 12m^3n - 9m^2$

Answer:

$6m^3 + 12m^3n - 9m^2$ $= 3m^2(2m + 4mn - 3)$	All the terms share the factor m^2, and 3 is the greatest common factor of 6, 12, and 9. So, the GCF is $3m^2$.

Factoring Trinomials

If the leading coefficient is $a = 1$, the trinomial is in the form $x^2 + bx + c$ and can often be rewritten in the factored form, as a product of two binomials: $(x + m)(x + n)$. Recall that the product of two binomials can be written in expanded form $x^2 + mx + nx + mn$. Equating this expression with $x^2 + bx + c$, the constant term c would have to equal the product mn. Thus, to work backward from the trinomial to the factored form, consider all the numbers m and n that multiply to make c. For example, to factor $x^2 + 8x + 12$, consider all the pairs that multiply to be 12 ($12 = 1 \times 12$ or 2×6 or 3×4). Choose the pair that will make the coefficient of the middle term (8) when added. In this example 2 and 6 add to 8, so making $m = 2$ and $n = 6$ in the expanded form gives:

$x^2 + 8x + 12 = x^2 + 2x + 6x + 12$	
$= (x^2 + 2x) + (6x + 12)$	Group the first two terms and the last two terms.
$= x(x + 6) + 2(x + 6)$	Factor the GCF out of each set of parentheses.

$= (x + 6)(x + 2)$ | The two terms now have the common factor $(x + 6)$, which can be removed, leaving $(x + 2)$ and the original polynomial is factored.

In general:

$x^2 + bx + c = x^2 + mx + nx + mn$, where $c = mn$ and $b = m + n$

$= (x^2 + mx) + (nx + mn)$	Group.
$= x(x + m) + n(x + m)$	Factor each group.
$= (x + m)(x + n)$	Factor out the common binomial.

Note that if none of the factors of c add to the value b, then the trinomial cannot be factored, and is called PRIME.

If the leading coefficient is not 1 ($a \neq 1$), first make sure that any common factors among the three terms are factored out. If the a-value is negative, factor out –1 first as well. If the a-value of the new polynomial in the parentheses is still not 1, follow this rule: Identify two values r and s that multiply to be ac and add to be b. Then write the polynomial in this form: $ax^2 + bx + c = ax^2 + rx + sx + c$, and proceed by grouping, factoring, and removing the common binomial as above.

There are a few special factoring cases worth memorizing: difference of squares, binomial squared, and the sum and difference of cubes.

- **Difference of squares** (each term is a square and they are subtracted):
  - $a^2 - b^2 = (a + b)(a - b)$
  - Note that a SUM of squares is never factorable.
- **Binomial squared**:
  - $a^2 + 2ab + b^2 = (a + b)(a + b) = (a + b)^2$
- **Sum and difference of cubes**:
  - $a^3 + b^3 = (a + b)(a^2 - ab + b^2)$
  - $a^3 - b^3 = (a - b)(a^2 + ab + b^2)$
  - Note that the second factor in these factorizations will never be able to be factored further.

EXAMPLES

1) Factor: $16x^2 + 52x + 30$

Answer:

$16x^2 + 52x + 30$	
$= 2(8x^2 + 26x + 15)$	Remove the GCF of 2.

	To factor the polynomial in the parentheses, calculate $ac = (8)(15) = 120$, and consider all the pairs of numbers that multiply to be 120: 1×120, 2×60, 3×40, 4×30, 5×24, 6×20, 8×15, and 10×12. Of these pairs, choose the pair that adds to be the b-value 26 (6 and 20).
$= 2(8x^2 + 6x + 20x + 15)$	
$= 2[(8x^2 + 6x) + (20x + 15)]$	Group.
$= 2[(2x(4x + 3) + 5(4x + 3)]$	Factor out the GCF of each group.
$= 2[(4x + 3)(2x + 5)]$	Factor out the common binomial.
$2(4x + 3)(2x + 5)$	

If there are no values r and s that multiply to be ac and add to be b, then the polynomial is prime and cannot be factored.

8) Factor $16x^2 + 52x + 30$

Answer:

$16x^2 + 52x + 30$	
$= 2(8x^2 + 26x + 15)$	Remove the GCF of 2.
$= 2(8x^2 + 6x + 20x + 15)$	Factor the polynomial in the parentheses. Calculate $ac = (8)(15) = 120$. Consider all the pairs of numbers that multiply to be 120: 1×120, 2×60, 3×40, 4×30, 5×24, 6×20, 8×15, and 10×12. Choose the pair that adds up to the b-value 26 (6 and 20).
$= 2[(8x^2 + 6x) + (20x + 15)]$	Group.
$= 2[(2x(4x + 3) + 5(4x + 3)]$	Factor out the GCF of each group.
$= 2(4x + 3)(2x + 5)$	Factor out the common binomial.

Linear Equations

An **EQUATION** states that two expressions are equal to each other. Polynomial equations are categorized by the highest power of the variables they contain: the highest power of any exponent of a linear equation is 1, a quadratic equation has a variable raised to the second power, a cubic equation has a variable raised to the third power, and so on.

Solving Linear Equations

Solving an equation means finding the value or values of the variable that make the equation true. To solve a linear equation, it is necessary to manipulate the terms so that the variable being solved for appears alone on one side of the equal sign while everything else in the equation is on the other side.

The way to solve linear equations is to "undo" all the operations that connect numbers to the variable of interest. Follow these steps:

1. Eliminate fractions by multiplying each side by the least common multiple of any denominators.
2. Distribute to eliminate parentheses, braces, and brackets.
3. Combine like terms.
4. Use addition or subtraction to collect all terms containing the variable of interest to one side, and all terms not containing the variable to the other side.
5. Use multiplication or division to remove coefficients from the variable of interest.

Sometimes there are no numeric values in the equation or there are a mix of numerous variables and constants. The goal is to solve the equation for one of the variables in terms of the other variables. In this case, the answer will be an expression involving numbers and letters instead of a numeric value.

On multiple choice tests, it is often easier to plug the possible values into the equation and determine which solution makes the equation true than to solve the equation.

EXAMPLES

1) Solve for x: $\dfrac{100(x+5)}{20} = 1$

Answer:

$\dfrac{100(x+5)}{20} = 1$	
$(20)\left(\dfrac{100(x+5)}{20}\right) = (1)(20)$ $100(x+5) = 20$	Multiply both sides by 20 to cancel out the denominator.
$100x + 500 = 20$	Distribute 100 through the parentheses.
$100x = -480$	"Undo" the +500 by subtracting 500 on both sides of the equation to isolate the variable term.
$x = \dfrac{-480}{100}$	"Undo" the multiplication by 100 by dividing by 100 on both sides to solve for x.
$x = \mathbf{-4.8}$	

2) Solve for x: $2(x+2)^2 - 2x^2 + 10 = 42$

Answer:

$2(x+2)^2 - 2x^2 + 10 = 42$

$2(x+2)(x+2) - 2x^2 + 10 = 42$	Eliminate the exponents on the left side.
$2(x^2 + 4x + 4) - 2x^2 + 10 = 42$	Apply FOIL.
$2x^2 + 8x + 8 - 2x^2 + 10 = 42$	Distribute the 2.
$8x + 18 = 42$	Combine like terms on the left-hand side.
$8x = 24$	Isolate the variable. "Undo" +18 by subtracting 18 on both sides.
$x = 3$	"Undo" multiplication by 8 by dividing both sides by 8.

3) Solve the equation for D: $\dfrac{A(3B + 2D)}{2N} = 5M - 6$

Answer:

$\dfrac{A(3B + 2D)}{2N} = 5M - 6$	
$3AB + 2AD = 10MN - 12N$	Multiply both sides by $2N$ to clear the fraction, and distribute the A through the parentheses.
$2AD = 10MN - 12N - 3AB$	Isolate the term with the D in it by moving $3AB$ to the other side of the equation.
$D = \dfrac{(10MN - 12N - 3AB)}{2A}$	Divide both sides by $2A$ to get D alone on the right-hand side.

Graphs of Linear Equations

The most common way to write a linear equation is **SLOPE-INTERCEPT FORM**, $y = mx + b$. In this equation, m is the slope, which describes how steep the line is, and b is the y-intercept. Slope is often described as "rise over run" because it is calculated as the difference in y-values (rise) over the difference in x-values (run). The slope of the line is also the rate of change of the dependent variable y with respect to the independent variable x. The y-intercept is the point where the line crosses the y-axis, or where x equals zero.

To graph a linear equation, identify the y-intercept and place that point on the y-axis. If the slope is not written as a fraction, make it a fraction by writing it over 1 $\left(\frac{m}{1}\right)$. Then use the slope to count up (or down, if negative) the "rise" part of the slope and over the "run" part of the slope to find a second point. These points can then be connected to draw the line.

To find the equation of a line, identify the y-intercept, if possible, on the graph and use two easily identifiable points to find the slope. If the y-intercept is not easily identified, identify the slope by choosing easily identifiable points; then choose one point on the graph, plug the point and the slope values into the equation, and solve for the missing value b.

Use the phrase "Begin, Move" to remember that b is the y-intercept (where to begin) and m is the slope (how the line moves).

slope-intercept form:
$y = mx + b$
slope:
$m = \dfrac{y_2 - y_1}{x_2 - x_1}$

- standard form: $Ax + By = C$
- $m = -\dfrac{A}{B}$
- $x\text{-intercept} = \dfrac{C}{A}$
- $y\text{-intercept} = \dfrac{C}{B}$

Another way to express a linear equation is standard form: $Ax + By = C$. In order to graph equations in this form, it is often easiest to convert them to point-slope form. Alternately, it is easy to find the x- or y-intercept from this form, and once these two points are known, a line can be drawn through them. To find the x-intercept, simply make $y = 0$ and solve for x. Similarly, to find the y-intercept, make $x = 0$ and solve for y.

EXAMPLES

1) What is the slope of the line whose equation is $6x - 2y - 8 = 0$?

Answer:

$6x - 2y - 8 = 0$	
$-2y = -6x + 8$ $y = \dfrac{-6x + 8}{-2}$ $y = 3x - 4$	Rearrange the equation into slope-intercept form by solving the equation for y.
$m = 3$	The slope is 3, the value attached to x.

2) What is the equation of the following line?

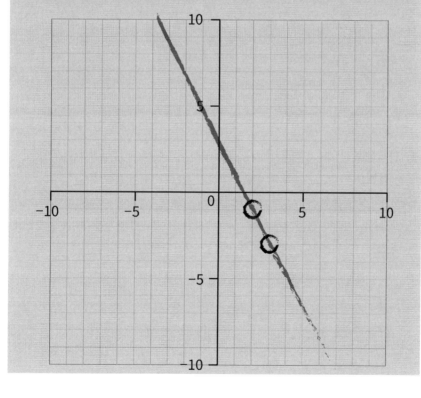

Answer:

$b = 3$	The y-intercept can be identified on the graph as $(0, 3)$.
$m = \dfrac{(-3) - (-1)}{3 - 2} = \dfrac{-2}{1} = -2$	To find the slope, choose any two points and plug the values into the slope equation. The two points chosen here are $(2, -1)$ and $(3, -3)$.
$y = -2x + 3$	Replace m with -2 and b with 3 in $y = mx + b$.

3) Write the equation of the line which passes through the points $(-2, 5)$ and $(-5, 3)$.

Answer:

$(-2, 5)$ and $(-5, 3)$	
$m = \dfrac{3 - 5}{(-5) - (-2)}$ $= \dfrac{-2}{-3}$ $= \dfrac{2}{3}$	Calculate the slope.
$5 = \dfrac{2}{3}(-2) + b$ $5 = \dfrac{-4}{3} + b$ $b = \dfrac{19}{3}$	To find b, plug into the equation $y = mx + b$ the slope for m and a set of points for x and y.
$y = \dfrac{2}{3}x + \dfrac{19}{3}$	Replace m and b to find the equation of the line.

4) What is the equation of the following graph?

Answer:

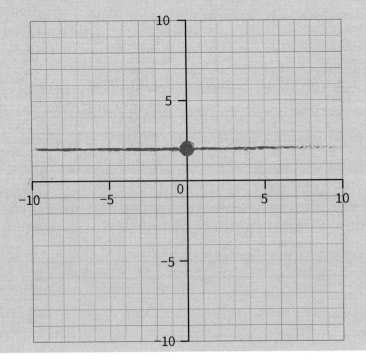

$y = 0x + 2$, or $y = 2$	The line has a rise of 0 and a run of 1, so the slope is $\frac{0}{1} = 0$. There is no x-intercept. The y-intercept is $(0, 2)$, meaning that the b-value in the slope-intercept form is 2.

Systems of Linear Equations

Systems of equations are sets of equations that include two or more variables. These systems can only be solved when there are at least as many equations as there are variables. Systems involve working with more than one equation to solve for more than one variable. For a system of linear equations, the solution to the system is the set of values for the variables that satisfies every equation in the system. Graphically, this will be the point where every line meets. If the lines are parallel (and hence do not intersect), the system will have no solution. If the lines are multiples of each other, meaning they share all coordinates, then the system has infinitely many solutions (because every point on the line is a solution).

Plug answers back into both equations to ensure the system has been solved properly.

one solution   **no solution**   **infinite solutions**

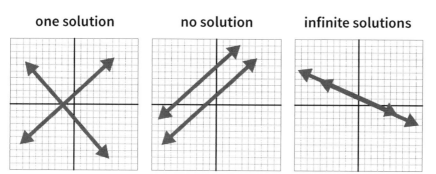

Figure 2.2. Systems of Equations

There are three common methods for solving systems of equations. To perform SUBSTITUTION, solve one equation for one variable, and then plug in the resulting expression for that variable in the second equation. This process works best for systems of two equations with two variables where the coefficient of one or more of the variables is 1.

To solve using ELIMINATION, add or subtract two equations so that one or more variables are eliminated. It's often necessary to multiply one or both of the equations by a scalar (constant) in order to make the variables cancel. Equations can be added or subtracted as many times as necessary to find each variable.

Yet another way to solve a system of linear equations is to use a MATRIX EQUATION. In the matrix equation $AX = B$, A contains the system's coefficients, X contains the variables, and B contains the constants (as shown below). The matrix equation can then be solved by multiplying B by the inverse of A: $X = A^{-1}B$

$$\begin{array}{l} ax + by = e \\ cx + dy = f \end{array} \rightarrow A = \begin{bmatrix} a & b \\ c & d \end{bmatrix} \quad X = \begin{bmatrix} x \\ y \end{bmatrix} \quad B = \begin{bmatrix} e \\ f \end{bmatrix} \rightarrow AX = B$$

This method can be extended to equations with three or more variables. Technology (such as a graphing calculator) is often employed when solving using this method if more than two variables are involved.

EXAMPLES

1) Solve for x and y:

$$2x - 4y = 28$$
$$4x - 12y = 36$$

Answer:

$2x - 4y = 28$ $x = 2y + 14$	Solve the system with substitution. Solve one equation for one variable.
$4x - 12y = 36$ $4(2y + 14) - 12y = 36$ $8y + 56 - 12y = 36$ $-4y = -20$ $y = 5$	Plug in the resulting expression for x in the second equation and simplify.
$2x - 4y = 28$ $2x - 4(5) = 28$ $2x - 20 = 28$ $2x = 48$ $x = 24$ The answer is $y = 5$ and $x = 24$ or **(24, 5)**.	Plug the solved variable into either equation to find the second variable.

2) Solve for the system for x and y:

$$3 = -4x + y$$
$$16x = 4y + 2$$

Answer:

$3 = -4x + y$ $y = 4x + 3$	Isolate the variable in one equation.
$16x = 4y + 2$ $16x = 4(4x + 3) + 2$ $16x = 16x + 12 + 2$ $0 = 14$ **No solution exists.**	Plug the expression into the second equation. Both equations have slope 4. This means the graphs of the equations are parallel lines, so no intersection (solution) exists.

3) Solve the system of equations:

$6x + 10y = 18$

$4x + 15y = 37$

Answer:

Because solving for x or y in either equation will result in messy fractions, this problem is best solved using elimination. The goal is to eliminate one of the variables by making the coefficients in front of one set of variables the same, but with different signs, and then adding both equations.

$6x + 10y = 18 \xrightarrow[(-2)]{} {}^{-12}x {}^{-20}y = {}^{-36}$ $4x + 15y = 37 \xrightarrow[(3)]{} {}^{12}x {}^{+45}y = {}^{1}\underline{11}$	To eliminate the x's in this problem, find the least common multiple of coefficients 6 and 4. The smallest number that both 6 and 4 divide into evenly is 12. Multiply the top equation by −2, and the bottom equation by 3.
$25y = 75$	Add the two equations to eliminate the x's.
$y = 3$	Solve for y.
$6x + 10(3) = 18$ $6x + 30 = 18$ $x = -2$	Replace y with 3 in either of the original equations.
The solution is **(−2, 3).**	

4) Solve the following systems of equations using matrix arithmetic:

$2x - 3y = -5$

$3x - 4y = -8$

Answer:

$\begin{bmatrix} 2 & -3 \\ 3 & -4 \end{bmatrix} \begin{bmatrix} x \\ y \end{bmatrix} = \begin{bmatrix} -5 \\ -8 \end{bmatrix}$	Write the system in matrix form, $\boldsymbol{AX = B}$.
$\begin{bmatrix} 2 & -3 \\ 3 & -4 \end{bmatrix}^{-1}$ $= \dfrac{1}{(2)(-4)-(-3)(3)} \begin{bmatrix} -4 & 3 \\ -3 & 2 \end{bmatrix} =$ $\begin{bmatrix} -4 & 3 \\ -3 & 2 \end{bmatrix}$	Calculate the inverse of Matrix $\boldsymbol{A}$.
$\begin{bmatrix} x \\ y \end{bmatrix} = \begin{bmatrix} -4 & 3 \\ -3 & 2 \end{bmatrix} \begin{bmatrix} -5 \\ -8 \end{bmatrix} = \begin{bmatrix} -4 \\ -1 \end{bmatrix}$	Multiply $\boldsymbol{B}$ by the inverse of $\boldsymbol{A}$.
$x = -4$ $y = -1$	Match up the 2 × 1 matrices to identify x and y.

Building Equations

Use the acronym STAR to remember word-problem strategies: Search the problem, Translate into an expression or equation, Answer, and Review.

In word problems, it is often necessary to translate a verbal description of a relationship into a mathematical equation. No matter the problem, this process can be done using the same steps:

1. Read the problem carefully and identify what value needs to be solved for.
2. Identify the known and unknown quantities in the problem, and assign the unknown quantities a variable.
3. Create equations using the variables and known quantities.
4. Solve the equations.
5. Check the solution: Does it answer the question asked in the problem? Does it make sense?

EXAMPLES

1) A school is holding a raffle to raise money. There is a $3 entry fee, and each ticket costs $5. If a student paid $28, how many tickets did he buy?

Answer:

Number of tickets = x Cost per ticket = 5 Cost for x tickets = $5x$ Total cost = 28 Entry fee = 3	Identify the quantities.
$5x + 3 = 28$	Set up equations. The total cost for x tickets will be equal to the cost for x tickets plus the $3 flat fee.
$5x + 3 = 28$ $5x = 25$ $x = 5$ The student bought **5 tickets**.	Solve the equation for x.

2) Kelly is selling shirts for her school swim team. There are two prices: a student price and a nonstudent price. During the first week of the sale, Kelly raised $84 by selling 10 shirts to students and 4 shirts to nonstudents. She earned $185 in the second week by selling 20 shirts to students and 10 shirts to nonstudents. What is the student price for a shirt?

Answer:

Student price = s Nonstudent price = n	Assign variables.

$10s + 4n = 84$ $20s + 10n = 185$	Create two equations using the number of shirts Kelly sold and the money she earned.
$10s + 4n = 84$ $10n = -20s + 185$ $n = -2s + 18.5$ $10s + 4(-2s + 18.5) = 84$ $10s - 8s + 74 = 84$ $2s + 74 = 84$ $2s = 10$ $s = 5$	Solve the system of equations using substitution.
The student cost for shirts is **$5**.	

Linear Inequalities

Solving Linear Inequalities

An inequality shows the relationship between two expressions, much like an equation. However, the equal sign is replaced with an inequality symbol that expresses the following relationships:

- ◆ < less than
- ◆ ≤ less than or equal to
- ◆ > greater than
- ◆ ≥ greater than or equal to

Inequalities are read from left to right. For example, the inequality $x \leq 8$ would be read as "x is less than or equal to 8," meaning x has a value smaller than or equal to 8. The set of solutions of an inequality can be expressed using a number line. The shaded region on the number line represents the set of all the numbers that make an inequality true. One major difference between equations and inequalities is that equations generally have a finite number of solutions, while inequalities generally have infinitely many solutions (an entire interval on the number line containing infinitely many values).

$x = 5$

Figure 2.3. Inequalities on a Number Line

Linear inequalities can be solved in the same way as linear equations, with one exception. When multiplying or dividing both sides of an inequality by a negative number, the direction of the inequality sign must reverse—"greater than" becomes "less than" and "less than" becomes "greater than."

EXAMPLES

1) Solve for z: $3z + 10 < -z$

Answer:

$3z + 10 < -z$	
$3z < -z - 10$	Collect nonvariable terms to one side.
$4z < -10$	Collect variable terms to the other side.
$z < -2.5$	Isolate the variable.

−2.5

2) Solve for x: $2x - 3 > 5(x - 4) - (x - 4)$

Answer:

$2x - 3 > 5(x - 4) - (x - 4)$	
$2x - 3 > 5x - 20 - x + 4$	Distribute 5 through the parentheses and −1 through the parentheses.
$2x - 3 > 4x - 16$	Combine like terms.
$-2x > -13$	Collect x-terms to one side, and constant terms to the other side.
$x < 6.5$	Divide both sides by −2; since dividing by a negative, reverse the direction of the inequality.

6.5

Compound Inequalities

Compound inequalities have more than one inequality expression. Solutions of compound inequalities are the sets of all numbers that make *all* the inequalities true. Some compound inequalities may not have any solutions, some will have solutions that contain some part of the number line, and some will have solutions that include the entire number line.

Table 2.1. Unions and Intersections

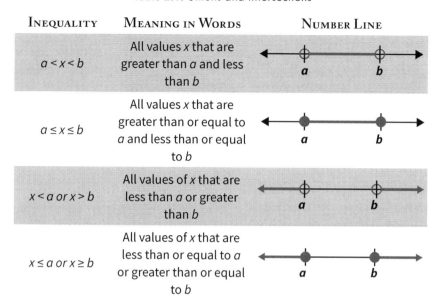

INEQUALITY	MEANING IN WORDS	NUMBER LINE
$a < x < b$	All values x that are greater than a and less than b	
$a \leq x \leq b$	All values x that are greater than or equal to a and less than or equal to b	
$x < a \ or \ x > b$	All values of x that are less than a or greater than b	
$x \leq a \ or \ x \geq b$	All values of x that are less than or equal to a or greater than or equal to b	

Compound inequalities can be written, solved, and graphed as two separate inequalities. For compound inequalities in which the word *and* is used, the solution to the compound inequality will be the set of numbers on the number line where both inequalities have solutions (where both are shaded). For compound inequalities where *or* is used, the solution to the compound inequality will be *all* the shaded regions for *either* inequality.

EXAMPLES

1) Solve the compound inequalities: $2x + 4 < -18 \ or \ 4(x + 2) > 18$

   Answer:

   $2x + 4 < -10 \ or \ 4(x + 2) > 18$

$2x < -14 \qquad 4x + 8 > 18$	
$x < -7 \qquad\ \ 4x > 10$	Solve each inequality independently.
$\qquad\qquad\ \ x > 2.5$	

   The solution to the original compound inequality is **the set of all x for which $x < -7$ or $x > 2.5$.**

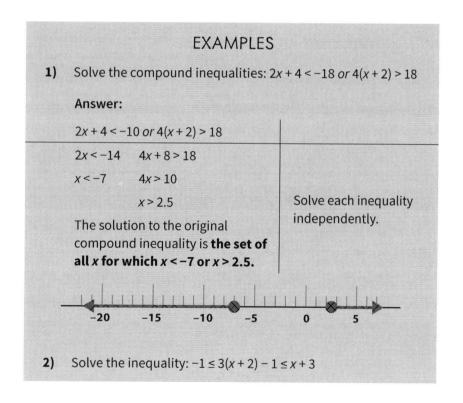

2) Solve the inequality: $-1 \leq 3(x + 2) - 1 \leq x + 3$

Answer:

$-1 \leq 3(x + 2) - 1 \leq x + 3$	
$-1 \leq 3(x + 2) - 1$ *and* $3(x + 2) - 1 \leq x + 3$	Break up the compound inequality into two inequalities.
$\begin{aligned} -1 &\leq 3x + 6 - 1 \quad\quad 3x + 6 - 1 \leq x + 3 \\ -6 &\leq 3x \quad\quad\quad\quad\quad 2x \leq -2 \\ -2 &\leq x \quad\quad\text{and}\quad x \leq -1 \end{aligned}$	Solve separately.
$\mathbf{-2 \leq x \leq -1}$	The only values of x that satisfy *both* inequalities are the values between −2 and −1 (inclusive).

Graphing Linear Inequalities in Two Variables

Linear inequalities in two variables can be graphed in much the same way as linear equations. Start by graphing the corresponding equation of a line (temporarily replace the inequality with an equal sign, and then graph). This line creates a boundary line of two half-planes. If the inequality is a "greater/less than," the boundary should not be included and a dotted line is used. A solid line is used to indicate that the boundary should be included in the solution when the inequality is "greater/less than or equal to."

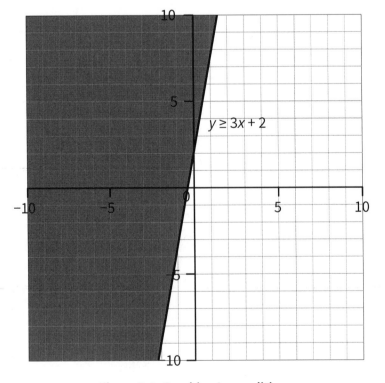

Figure 2.4. Graphing Inequalities

One side of the boundary is the set of all points (x, y) that make the inequality true. This side is shaded to indicate that all these values are solutions. If y is greater than the expression containing x, shade above the line; if it is less than, shade below. A point can also be used to check which side of the line to shade.

A set of two or more linear inequalities is a **SYSTEM OF INEQUALITIES**. Solutions to the system are all the values of the variables that make every inequality in the system true. Systems of inequalities are solved graphically by graphing all the inequalities in the same plane. The region where all the shaded solutions overlap is the solution to the system.

A dotted line is used for "greater/less than" because the solution may approach that line, but the coordinates on the line can never be a solution.

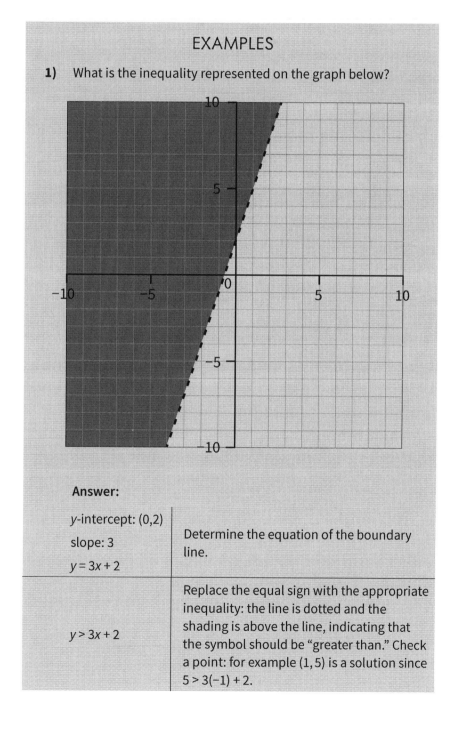

EXAMPLES

1) What is the inequality represented on the graph below?

Answer:

y-intercept: (0,2) slope: 3 $y = 3x + 2$	Determine the equation of the boundary line.
$y > 3x + 2$	Replace the equal sign with the appropriate inequality: the line is dotted and the shading is above the line, indicating that the symbol should be "greater than." Check a point: for example $(1, 5)$ is a solution since $5 > 3(-1) + 2$.

2) Graph the following inequality: $3x + 6y \leq 12$.

Answer:

$3x + 6y \leq 12$	
$3(0) + 6y = 12$	
$y = 2$	
y-intercept: $(0, 2)$	Find the x- and y-intercepts.
$3x + 6(0) \leq 12$	
$x = 4$	
x-intercept: $(4, 0)$	

Graph the line using the intercepts, and shade below the line.

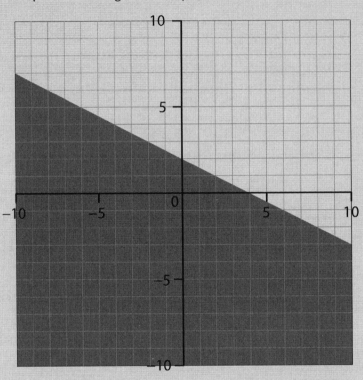

3) Graph the system of inequalities: $-x + y \leq 1, x \geq -1, y > 2x - 4$

Answer:

To solve the system, graph all three inequalities in the same plane; then identify the area where the three solutions overlap. All points (x, y) in this area will be solutions to the system since they satisfy all three inequalities.

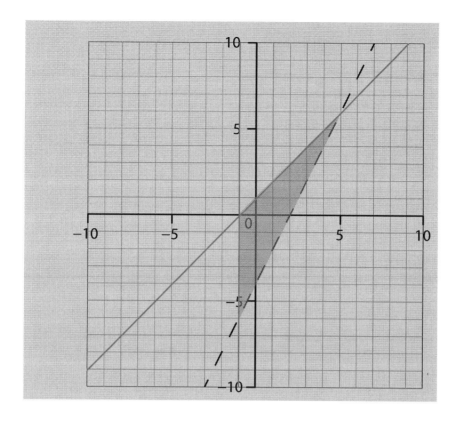

Quadratic Equations and Inequalities

Quadratic equations are degree 2 polynomials; the highest power on the dependent variable is two. While linear functions are represented graphically as lines, the graph of a quadratic function is a PARABOLA. The graph of a parabola has three important components. The VERTEX is where the graph changes direction. In the parent graph $y = x^2$, the origin $(0, 0)$ is the vertex. The AXIS OF SYMMETRY is the vertical line that cuts the graph into two equal halves. The line of symmetry always passes through the vertex. On the parent graph, the y-axis is the axis of symmetry. The ZEROS or ROOTS of the quadratic are the x-intercepts of the graph.

Forms of Quadratic Equations

Quadratic equations can be expressed in two forms:

- STANDARD FORM: $y = ax^2 + bx + c$

  Axis of symmetry: $x = -\frac{b}{2a}$ Vertex: $(-\frac{b}{2a}, f(-\frac{b}{2a}))$

- VERTEX FORM: $y = a(x - h)^2 + k$

  Vertex: (h, k) Axis of symmetry: $x = h$

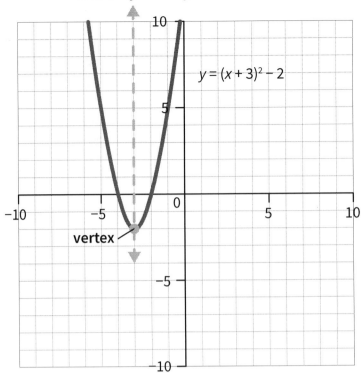

axis of symmetry

$y = (x + 3)^2 - 2$

vertex

Figure 2.5. Parabola

In both equations, the sign of *a* determines which direction the parabola opens: if *a* is positive, then it opens upward; if *a* is negative, then it opens downward. The wideness or narrowness is also determined by *a*. If the absolute value of *a* is less than one (a proper fraction), then the parabola will get wider the closer |*a*| is to zero. If the absolute value of *a* is greater than one, then the larger |*a*| becomes, the narrower the parabola will be.

Equations in vertex form can be converted to standard form by squaring out the $(x - h)^2$ part (using FOIL), distributing the *a*, adding *k*, and simplifying the result.

Equations can be converted from standard form to vertex form by COMPLETING THE SQUARE. Take an equation in standard form, $y = ax^2 + bc + c$.

1. Move *c* to the left side of the equation.
2. Divide the entire equation through by *a* (to make the coefficient of x^2 be 1).
3. Take half of the coefficient of *x*, square that number, and then add the result to both sides of the equation.

4. Convert the right side of the equation to a perfect binomial squared, $(x + m)^2$.

5. Isolate y to put the equation in proper vertex form.

EXAMPLES

1) What is the line of symmetry for $y = -2(x + 3)^2 + 2$?

Answer:

This quadratic is given in vertex form, with $h = -3$ and $k = 2$. The vertex of this equation is $(-3, 2)$. The line of symmetry is the vertical line that passes through this point. Since the x-value of the point is -3, the line of symmetry is **$x = -3$**.

2) What is the vertex of the parabola $y = -3x^2 + 24x - 27$?

Answer:

$y = -3x^2 + 24x - 27$	
$x = -\dfrac{b}{2a}$ where $a = -3$, $b = 24$ $x = \dfrac{24}{2(-3)} = 4$	This quadratic equation is in standard form. Use the formula for finding the x-value of the vertex.
$y = -3(4)^2 + 24(4) - 27 = 21$ The vertex is at **(4, 21)**.	Plug $x = 4$ into the original equation to find the corresponding y-value.

3) Write $y = -3x^2 + 24x - 27$ in vertex form by completing the square.

Answer:

$y = -3x^2 + 24x - 27$	
$y + 27 = -3x^2 + 24x$	Move c to the other side of the equation.
$\dfrac{y}{-3} - 9 = x^2 - 8x$	Divide through by a (-3 in this example).
$\dfrac{y}{-3} - 9 + 16 = x^2 - 8x + 16$	Take half of the new b, square it, and add that quantity to both sides: $\frac{1}{2}(-8) = -4$. Squaring it gives $(-4)^2 = 16$.
$\dfrac{y}{-3} + 7 = (x - 4)^2$	Simplify the left side, and write the right side as a binomial squared.
$y = -3(x - 4)^2 + 21$	Subtract 7, and then multiply through by -3 to isolate y.

Solving Quadratic Equations

Solving the quadratic equation $ax^2 + bx + c = 0$ finds x-intercepts of the parabola (by making $y = 0$). These are also called the ROOTS or ZEROS of the quadratic function. A quadratic equation may have zero, one, or two real solutions. There are several ways of finding the zeros. One way is to factor the quadratic into a product of two binomials, and then use the zero product property. (If $m \times n = 0$, then either $m = 0$ or $n = 0$.) Another way is to complete the square and square root both sides. One way that works every time is to memorize and use the **QUADRATIC FORMULA**:

$$x = \frac{-b \pm \sqrt{b^2 - 4ac}}{2a}$$

The a, b, and c come from the standard form of quadratic equations above. (Note that to use the quadratic equation, the right-hand side of the equation must be equal to zero.)

The part of the formula under the square root radical ($b^2 - 4ac$) is known as the **DISCRIMINANT**. The discriminant tells how many and what type of roots will result without actually calculating the roots.

With all graphing problems, putting the function into the $y =$ window of a graphing calculator will aid the process of elimination when graphs are examined and compared to answer choices with a focus on properties like axis of symmetry, vertices, and roots of formulas.

Table 2.2. Discriminants

IF $B^2 - 4AC$ IS	THERE WILL BE	AND THE PARABOLA
zero	only 1 real root	has its vertex on the x-axis
positive	2 real roots	has **two** x-intercepts
negative	0 real roots 2 complex roots	has **no** x-intercepts

EXAMPLES

1) Find the zeros of the quadratic equation: $y = -(x + 3)^2 + 1$.

Answer:

Method 1: Make $y = 0$; isolate x by square rooting both sides:

$0 = -(x + 3)^2 + 1$	Make $y = 0$.
$-1 = -(x + 3)^2$	Subtract 1 from both sides.
$1 = (x + 3)^2$	Divide by -1 on both sides.
$(x + 3) = \pm 1$	Square root both sides. Don't forget to write plus OR minus 1.
$(x + 3) = 1$ or $(x + 3) = -1$	Write two equations using $+1$ and -1.
$x = -2$ or $x = -4$	Solve both equations. These are the zeros.

Method 2: Convert vertex form to standard form, and then use the quadratic formula.

$y = -(x + 3)^2 + 1$ $y = -(x^2 + 6x + 9) + 1$ $y = -x^2 - 6x - 8$	Put the equation in standard form by distributing and combining like terms.
$x = \dfrac{-b \pm \sqrt{(b^2 - 4ac)}}{2a}$ $x = \dfrac{-(-6) \pm \sqrt{(-6)^2 - 4(-1)(-8)}}{2(-1)}$ $x = \dfrac{6 \pm \sqrt{36 - 32}}{-2}$ $x = \dfrac{6 \pm \sqrt{4}}{-2}$ $x = -4, -2$	Find the zeros using the quadratic formula.

33) Find the root(s) for: $z^2 - 4z + 4 = 0$

Answer:

This polynomial can be factored in the form $(z - 2)(z - 2) = 0$, so the only root is $z = 2$. There is only one x-intercept, and the vertex of the graph is *on* the x-axis.

34) Write a quadratic function that has zeros at $x = -3$ and $x = 2$ that passes through the point $(-2, 8)$.

Answer:

If the quadratic has zeros at $x = -3$ and $x = 2$, then it has factors of $(x + 3)$ and $(x - 2)$. The quadratic function can be written in the factored form $y = a(x + 3)(x - 2)$. To find the a-value, plug in the point $(-2, 8)$ for x and y:

$8 = a(-2 + 3)(-2 - 2)$

$8 = a(-4)$

$a = -2$

The quadratic function is **$y = -2(x + 3)(x - 2)$**.

Graphing Quadratic Equations

The final expected quadratic skills are graphing a quadratic function given its equation and determining the equation of a quadratic function from its graph. The equation's form determines which quantities are easiest to obtain:

Table 2.3 Obtaining Quantities from Quadratic Functions

NAME OF FORM	EQUATION OF QUADRATIC	EASIEST QUANTITY TO FIND	HOW TO FIND OTHER QUANTITIES
vertex form	$y = a(x - h)^2 + k$	vertex at (h, k) and axis of symmetry $x = h$	Find zeros by making $y = 0$ and solving for x.

			Find axis of symmetry by averaging m and n: $x = \frac{m+n}{2}.$
factored form	$y = a(x - m)(x - n)$	x – intercepts at $x = m$ and $x = n$	This is also the x-value of the vertex.

Table 2.3 Obtaining Quantities from Quadratic Functions (continued)

NAME OF FORM	EQUATION OF QUADRATIC	EASIEST QUANTITY TO FIND	HOW TO FIND OTHER QUANTITIES
standard form	$y = ax^2 + bx + c$	y – intercept at $(0, c)$	Find axis of symmetry and x-value of the vertex using $x = \frac{-b}{2a}.$ Find zeros using quadratic formula.

To graph a quadratic function, first determine if the graph opens up or down by examining the a-value. Then determine the quantity that is easiest to find based on the form given, and find the vertex. Then other values can be found, if necessary, by choosing x-values and finding the corresponding y-values. Using symmetry instantly doubles the number of points that are known.

Given the graph of a parabola, the easiest way to write a quadratic equation is to identify the vertex and insert the h- and k-values into the vertex form of the equation. The a-value can be determined by finding another point the graph goes through, plugging these values in for x and y, and solving for a.

EXAMPLES

1) Graph the quadratic $y = 2(x - 3)^2 + 4$.

Answer:

Start by marking the vertex at $(3, 4)$ and recognizing this parabola opens upward. The line of symmetry is $x = 3$. Now, plug in an easy value for x to get one point on the curve; then use symmetry to find another point. In this case, choose $x = 2$ (one unit to the left of the line of symmetry) and solve for y:

$y = 2(2 - 3)^2 + 4$

$y = 2(1) + 4$

$y = 6$

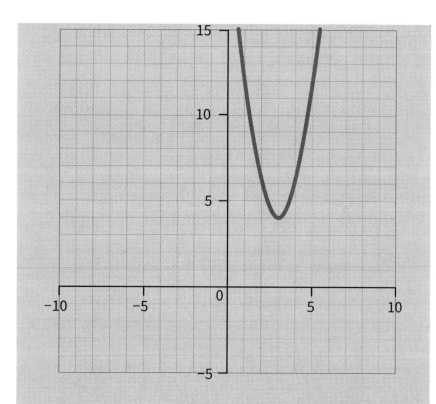

Thus the point $(2, 6)$ is on the curve. Then use symmetry to find the corresponding point one unit to the right of the line of symmetry, which must also have a y value of 6. This point is $(4, 6)$. Draw a parabola through the points.

2) What is the vertex form of the equation shown on the following graph?

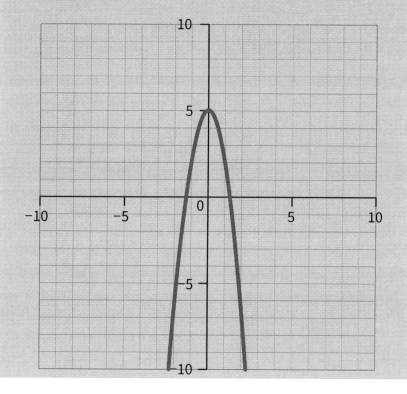

Answer:	
$(h, k) = (0, 5)$ $y = a(x - h)^2 + k$ $y = a(x - 0)^2 + 5$ $y = ax^2 + 5$	Locate the vertex and plug values for h and k into the vertex form of the quadratic equation.
$(x, y) = (1, 2)$ $y = ax^2 + 5$ $2 = a(1)^2 + 5$ $a = -3$	Choose another point on the graph to plug into this equation to solve for a.
$y = -3x^2 + 5$	Plug a into the vertex form of the equation.

Absolute Value Equations and Inequalities

The **ABSOLUTE VALUE** of a number means the distance between that number and zero. The absolute value of any number is positive since distance is always positive. The notation for absolute value of a number is two vertical bars:

$|-27| = 27$ The distance from –27 to 0 is 27.

$|27| = 27$ The distance from 27 to 0 is 27.

Solving equations and simplifying inequalities with absolute values usually requires writing two equations or inequalities, which are then solved separately using the usual methods of solving equations. To write the two equations, set one equation equal to the positive value of the expression inside the absolute value and the other equal to the negative value. Two inequalities can be written in the same manner. However, the inequality symbol should be flipped for the negative value.

The formal definition of the absolute value is

$$|x| = \begin{cases} -x, & x < 0 \\ x, & x \geq 0 \end{cases}$$

This is true because whenever x is negative, the opposite of x is the answer (for example, $|-5| = -(-5) = 5$, but when x is positive, the answer is just x. This type of function is called a **PIECE-WISE FUNCTION**. It is defined in two (or more) distinct pieces. To graph the absolute value function, graph each piece separately. When $x < 0$ (that is, when it is negative), graph the line $y = -x$. When $x > 0$ (that is, when x is positive), graph the line $y = x$. This creates a V-shaped graph that is the parent function for absolute value functions.

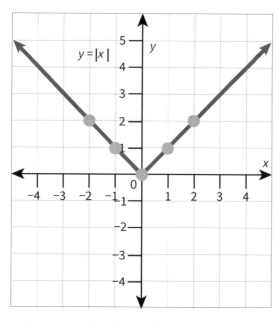

Figure 2.6. Absolute Value Parent Function

EXAMPLES

1) Solve for x: $|x - 3| = 27$

   Answer:

   Set the quantity inside the parentheses equal to 27 or −27, and solve:

$x - 3 = 27$	$x - 3 = -27$
$x = 30$	$x = -24$

2) Solve for r: $\frac{|r-7|}{5} = 27$

   Answer:

   The first step is to isolate the absolute value part of the equation. Multiplying both sides by 5 gives:

   $|r - 7| = 135$

   If the quantity in the absolute value bars is 135 or −135, then the absolute value would be 135:

$r - 7 = 135$	$r - 7 = -135$
$r = 142$	$r = -128$

3) Find the solution set for the following inequality: $\left|\frac{3x}{7}\right| \geq 4 - x$.

   Answer:

$\left|\frac{3x}{7}\right| \geq 4 - x$	
$\frac{|3x|}{7} \geq 4 - x$	
$|3x| \geq 28 - 7x$	Simplify the equation.

$3x \geq 28 - 7x$ $10x \geq 28$ $x \geq \frac{28}{10}$ $-(3x) \leq 28 - 7x$ $-3x \leq 28 - 7x$ $4x \leq 28$ $x \leq 7$	Create and solve two inequalities. When including the negative answer, flip the inequality.
$\frac{28}{10} \leq x \leq 7$	Combine the two answers to find the solution set.

Functions

Working with Functions

Functions can be thought of as a process: when something is put in, an action (or operation) is performed, and something different comes out. A **FUNCTION** is a relationship between two quantities (for example x and y) in which, for every value of the independent variable (usually x), there is exactly one value of the dependent variable (usually y). Briefly, each input has *exactly one* output. Graphically this means the graph passes the **VERTICAL LINE TEST**: anywhere a vertical line is drawn on the graph, the line hits the curve at exactly one point.

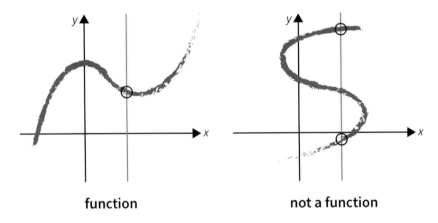

function   not a function

Figure 2.7. Vertical Line Test

The notation $f(x)$ or $g(t)$, etc., is often used when a function is being considered. This is **FUNCTION NOTATION**. The input value is x and the output value y is written as $y = f(x)$. Thus, $f(2)$ represents the output value (or y value) when $x = 2$, and $f(2) = 5$ means that when $x = 2$ is plugged into the $f(x)$ function, the output (y value) is 5. In other words, $f(2) = 5$ represents the point $(2, 5)$ on the graph of $f(x)$.

Every function has an **INPUT DOMAIN** and **OUTPUT RANGE**. The domain is the set of all the possible x values that can be used as input values (these are found along the horizontal axis on the graph), and the range includes all the *y* values or output values that result from applying *f*(*x*) (these are found along the vertical axis on the graph). Domain and range are usually intervals of numbers and are often expressed as inequalities, such as $x < 2$ (the domain is all values less than 2) or $3 < x < 15$ (all values between 3 and 15).

Interval notation can also be used to show domain and range. Round brackets indicate that an end value is not included, and square brackets show that it is. The symbol ∪ means *or*, and the symbol ∩ means *and*. For example, the statement (–infinity, 4) ∪ (4, infinity) describes the set of all real numbers except 4.

A function *f*(*x*) is **EVEN** if $f(-x) = f(x)$. Even functions have symmetry across the *y*-axis. An example of an even function is the parent quadratic $y = x^2$, because any value of *x* (for example, 3) and its opposite –*x* (for example, –3) have the same *y* value (for example, $3^2 = 9$ and $(-3)^2 = 9$). A function is **ODD** if $f(-x) = -f(x)$. Odd functions have symmetry about the origin. For example, $f(x) = x^3$ is an odd function because $f(3) = 27$, and $f(-3) = -27$. A function may be even, odd, or neither.

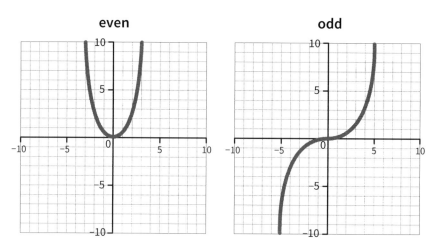

Figure 2.8. Even and Odd Functions

EXAMPLES

1) Evaluate: $f(4)$ if $f(x) = x^3 - 2x + \sqrt{x}$

Answer:

$f(x) = x^3 - 2x + \sqrt{x}$	
$f(4) = (4)^3 - 2(4) + \sqrt{(4)}$	Plug in 4.
$= 64 - 8 + 2$	Follow the PEMDAS order of operations.
$= \textbf{58}$	

2) What are the domain and range of the following function?

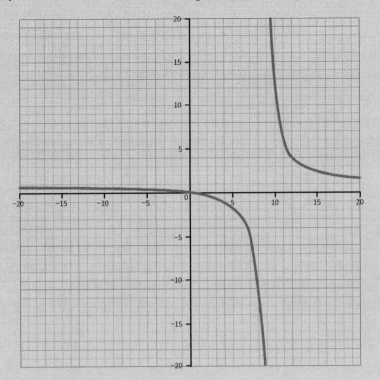

Answer:

This function has an asymptote at $x = 9$, so is not defined there. Otherwise, the function is defined for all other values of x.

D: $-\infty < x < 9$ or $9 < x < \infty$

Since the function has a horizontal asymptote at $y = 1$ that it never crosses, the function never takes the value 1, so the range is all real numbers except 1: **R:** $-\infty < y < 1$ or $1 < y < \infty$.

3) Which of the following represents a function?

A.

X	G(X)
0	0
1	1
2	2
1	3

B.

X	F(X)
0	1
0	2
0	3
0	4

C.

T	F(T)
1	1
2	2
3	3
4	4

D.

X	F(X)
0	0
5	1
0	2
5	3

Answer:

For a set of numbers to represent a function, every input must generate a unique output. Therefore, if the same input (x)

appears more than once in the table, determine if that input has two different outputs. If so, then the table does not represent a function.

A. This table is not a function because input value 1 has two different outputs (1 and 3).

B. Table B is not function because 0 is the only input and results in four different values.

C. This table shows a function because each input has one output.

D. This table also has one input going to two different values, so it is not a function.

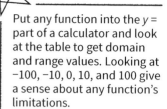
Put any function into the *y* = part of a calculator and look at the table to get domain and range values. Looking at −100, −10, 0, 10, and 100 give a sense about any function's limitations.

4) What is the domain and the range of the following graph?

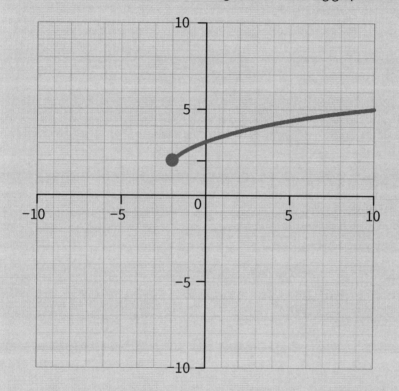

Answer:

For the domain, this graph goes on to the right to positive infinity. Its leftmost point, however, is *x* = −2. Therefore, its domain is all real numbers equal to or greater than −2, **D: − 2 ≤ *x* < ∞, or [−2, ∞).**

The lowest range value is *y* = 2. Although it has a decreasing slope, this function continues to rise. Therefore, the domain is all real numbers greater than 2, **R: 2 ≤ *y* < ∞ or [2, ∞).**

Inverse Functions

INVERSE FUNCTIONS switch the inputs and the outputs of a function. If $f(x) = k$ then the inverse of that function would read $f^{-1}(k) = x$. The domain of $f^{-1}(x)$ is the range of $f(x)$, and the range of $f^{-1}(x)$ is the domain of $f(x)$. If point (a, b) is on the graph of $f(x)$, then point (b, a) will be on

Inverse graphs can be tested by taking any point on one graph and flipping coordinates to see if that new point is on the other curve. For example, the coordinate point (5, −2) is on the function and (−2, 5) is a point on its inverse.

the graph of $f^{-1}(x)$. Because of this fact, the graph of $f^{-1}(x)$ is a reflection of the graph of $f(x)$ across the line $y = x$. Inverse functions "undo" all the operations of the original function.

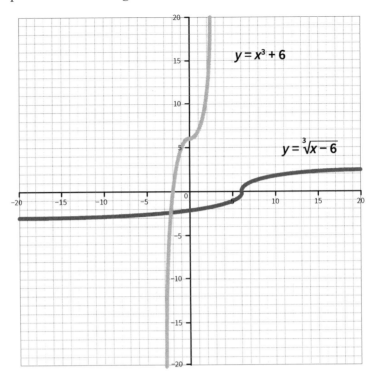

Figure 2.9. Inverse Functions

The steps for finding an inverse function are:
1. Replace $f(x)$ with y to make it easier manipulate the equation.
2. Switch the x and y.
3. Solve for y.
4. Label the inverse function as $f^{-1}(x) =$.

EXAMPLESS

1) What is the inverse of function of $f(x) = 5x + 5$?

Answer:

$y = 5x + 5$	Replace $f(x)$ with y
$x = 5y + 5$	Switch the places of y and x.
$x = 5y + 5$	
$x - 5 = 5y$	Solve for y.
$y = \frac{x}{5} - 1$	
$f^{-1}(x) = \frac{x}{5} - 1$	

2) Find the inverse of the graph of $f(x) = -1 - \frac{1}{5}x$

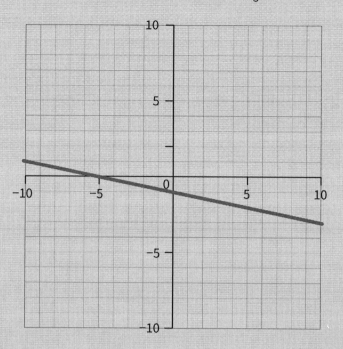

Answer:

This is a linear graph with some clear coordinates: $(-5, 0)$, $(0, -1)$, $(5, -2)$, and $(10, -3)$. This means the inverse function will have coordinate $(0, -5)$, $(-1, 0)$, $(-2, 5)$, and $(-3, 10)$. The inverse function is reflected over the line $y = x$ and is the line $f^{-1}(x) = -5(x + 1)$ below.

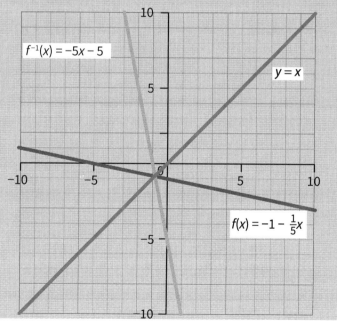

Compound Functions

COMPOUND FUNCTIONS take two or more functions and combine them using operations or composition. Functions can be combined using addition, subtraction, multiplication, or division:

$$\text{addition: } (f + g)(x) = f(x) + g(x)$$

$$\text{subtraction: } (f - g)(x) = f(x) - g(x)$$

$$\text{multiplication: } (fg)(x) = f(x)g(x)$$

$$\text{division: } \left(\frac{f}{g}\right)(x) = \frac{f(x)}{g(x)} \text{ (note that } g(x) \neq 0)$$

Functions can also be combined using COMPOSITION. Composition of functions is indicated by the notation $(f \circ g)(x)$. Note that the $\circ$ symbol does NOT mean multiply. It means take the output of $g(x)$ and make it the input of $f(x)$:

$$(f \circ g)(x) = f(g(x))$$

This equation is read f of g of x, and will be a new function of x. Note that order is important. In general, $f(g(x)) \neq g(f(x))$. They *will* be equal when $f(x)$ and $g(x)$ are inverses of each other, however, as both will simplify to the original input x. This is because performing a function on a value and then using that output as the input to the inverse function should bring you back to the original value.

The domain of a composition function is the set of x values that are in the domain of the "inside" function $g(x)$ such that $g(x)$ is in the domain of the outside function $f(x)$. For example, if $f(x) = \frac{1}{x}$ and $g(x) = \sqrt{x}$, $f(g(x))$ has a domain of $x > 0$ because $g(x)$ has a domain of $x \geq 0$. But when $f(x)$ is applied to the $\sqrt{x}$ function, the composition function becomes $\frac{1}{\sqrt{x}}$ and the value $x = 0$ is no longer allowed because it would result in 0 in the denominator, so the domain must be further restricted.

EXAMPLES

1) If $z(x) = 3x - 3$ and $y(x) = 2x - 1$, find $(y \circ z)(-4)$.

Answer:

$(y \circ z)(-4) = y(z(-4))$	
$z(-4)$	
$= 3(-4) - 3$	Starting on the inside, evaluate z.
$= -12 - 3$	
$= -15$	

$$y(z(-4))$$

$$= y(-15)$$

$$= 2(-15) - 1$$ Replace $z(-4)$ with -15, and simplify.

$$= -30 - 1$$

$$\mathbf{= -31}$$

2) Find $(k \circ t)(x)$ if $k(x) = \frac{1}{2}x - 3$ and $t(x) = \frac{1}{2}x - 2$.

Answer:

$(k \circ t)(x) = k(t(x))$ $= k\left(\frac{1}{2}x - 2\right)$ $= \frac{1}{2}\left(\frac{1}{2}x - 2\right) - 3$	Replace x in the $k(x)$ function with $\left(\frac{1}{2}x - 2\right)$
$= \frac{1}{4}x - 1 - 3$ $= \frac{1}{4}x - 4$	Simplify.

$$\mathbf{(k \circ t)(x) = \frac{1}{4}x - 4}$$

3) The wait (W) to get on a ride at an amusement park depends on the number of people (N) in the park. The number of people in the park depends on the number of hours, t, that the park has been open. Suppose $N(t) = 400t$ and $W(N) = 5(1.2)\frac{N}{100}$. What is the value and the meaning in context of $N(4)$ and $W(N(4))$?

Answer:

$N(4) = 400(4) = 1600$ and means that 4 hours after the park opens there are 1600 people in the park. $W(N(4)) = W(1600) = 96$ and means that 4 hours after the park opens the wait time is about **96 minutes** for the ride.

Transforming Functions

Many functions can be graphed using simple transformation of parent functions. Transformations include reflections across axes, vertical and horizontal translations (or shifts), and vertical or horizontal stretches or compressions. The table gives the effect of each transformation to the graph of any function $y = f(x)$.

Table 2.4. Effects of Transformations

EQUATION	EFFECT ON GRAPH
$y = -f(x)$	reflection across the x-axis (vertical reflection)
$y = f(x) + k$	vertical shift up k units ($k > 0$) or down k units ($k < 0$)
$y = kf(x)$	vertical stretch (if $k > 1$) or compression (if $k < 1$)

Table 2.4. Effects of Transformations (continued)

EQUATION	EFFECT ON GRAPH
$y = f(-x)$	reflection across the y-axis (horizontal reflection)
$y = f(x + k)$	horizontal shift right k units ($k < 0$) or left k units ($k > 0$)
$y = f(kx)$	horizontal stretch ($k < 1$) or compression ($k > 1$)

Note that the first three equations have an operation applied to the *outside* of the function $f(x)$ and these all cause *vertical changes* to the graph of the function that are *intuitive* (for example, adding a value moves it up). The last three equations have an operation applied to the *inside* of the function $f(x)$ and these all cause *horizontal changes* to the graph of the function that are *counterintuitive* (for example, multiplying the x's by a fraction results in stretch, not compression, which would seem more intuitive). It is helpful to group these patterns together to remember how each transformation affects the graph.

EXAMPLES

1) Graph: $y = |x + 1| + 4$

   Answer:

   This function is the absolute value function with a vertical shift up of 4 units (since the 4 is outside the absolute value bars), and a horizontal shift left of 1 unit (since it is inside the bars). The vertex of the graph is at $(-1, 4)$ and the line $x = -1$ is an axis of symmetry.

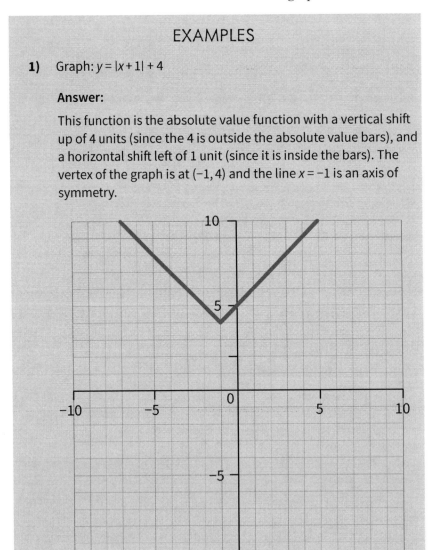

2) Graph: $y = -3|x - 2| + 2$

Answer:

The negative sign in front of the absolute value means the graph will be reflected across the *x*-axis, so it will open down. The 3 causes a vertical stretch of the function, which results in a narrower graph. The basic curve is shifted 2 units right (since the -2 is an inside change) and 2 units up (since the +2 is an outside change), so the vertex is at (2, 2).

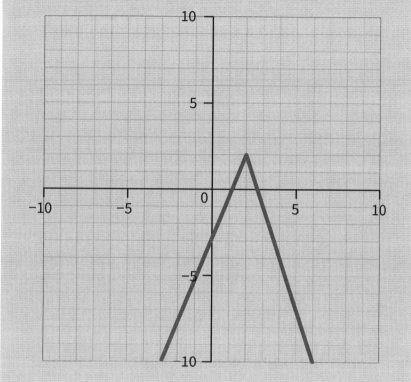

Exponential Functions

An **EXPONENTIAL FUNCTION** has a constant base and a variable in the exponent: $f(x) = b^x$ is an exponential function with base b and exponent x. The value b is the quantity that the y value is multiplied by each time the x value is increased by 1. When looking at a table of values, an exponential function can be identified because the $f(x)$ values are being multiplied. (In contrast, linear $f(x)$ values are being added to.)

The graph of the exponential parent function does not cross the x-axis, which is the function's horizontal asymptote. The y-intercept of the function is at (0, 1).

The general formula for an exponential function, $f(x) = ab^{(x-h)} + k$, allows for transformations to be made to the function. The value h moves the function left or right (moving the y-intercept) while the value k moves the function up or down (moving both the y-intercept and the horizontal asymptote). The value a stretches or compresses the function (moving the y-intercept).

To solve an exponential equation, start by looking for a common base:
$4^{x-2} = \sqrt{8}$
can be rewritten as
$(2^2)^{(x-2)} = (2^3)^{\frac{1}{2}}$
If no common base can be found, logarithms can be used to move the variable out of the exponent position.

Exponential equations have at least one variable in an exponent position. One way to solve these equations is to make the bases on both side of the equation equivalent, and then equate the exponents. Many exponential equations do not have a solution. Negative numbers often lead to no solutions: for example, $2^x = -8$. The domain of exponential functions is only positive numbers, as seen above, so there is no x value that will result in a negative output.

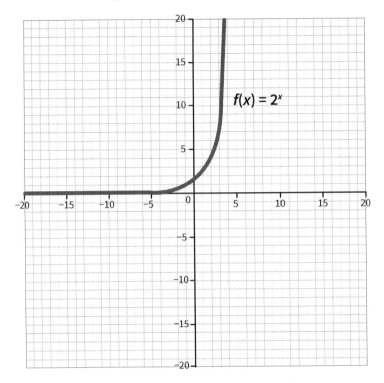

Figure 2.10. Exponential Parent Function

EXAMPLES

1) Graph the exponential function $f(x) = 5^x - 2$.

Answer:

One way to do this is to use a table:

x	$5^x - 2$
-2	$\frac{1}{25} - 2 = -\frac{49}{25}$
-1	$\frac{1}{5} - 2 = -\frac{9}{5}$
0	$1 - 2 = -1$
1	$5 - 2 = 3$
2	$25 - 2 = 23$

Another way to graph this is simply to see this function as the parent function $y = b^x$ (with $b = 5$), shifted down by a vertical shift of 2 units. Thus the new horizontal asymptote will be at $y = 2$, and the new y-intercept will be $y = -1$.

2) If the height of grass in a yard in a humid summer week grows by 5% every day, how much taller would the grass be after six days?

Answer:

Any time a question concerns growth or decay, an exponential function must be created to solve it. In this case, create a table with initial value a, and a daily growth rate of $(1+0.05) = 1.05$ per day.

Days (x)	Height (h)
0	a
1	$1.05a$
2	$1.05(1.05a) = (1.05)^2a$
3	$(1.05)^2(1.05a) = (1.05)^3a$
x	$(1.05)^xa$

After six days the height of the grass is $(1.05)^6 = $ **1.34 times as tall**. The grass would grow 34% in one week. Use 6 days because the table starts at 0, not 1.

3) Solve for x: $4^{x+1} = \frac{1}{256}$

Answer:

$4^{x+1} = \dfrac{1}{256}$	
$4^{x+1} = 4^{-4}$	Find a common base and rewrite the equation.
$x + 1 = -4$ $x = -5$	Set the exponents equal and solve for x.

Special Exponential Equations

There are three exponential function formulas that frequently show up in word problems:

The GROWTH FORMULA:

$y = a(1 + r)^t$ Initial amount a increases at a rate of r per time period

The DECAY FORMULA:

$y = a(1 - r)^t$ Initial amount a decreases at a rate of r per time period

In these formulas, a is the initial amount (at time $t = 0$), r is the rate of growth or decay (written as a decimal in the formula), and t is the number of growth or decay cycles that have passed.

A special case of the growth function is known as the COMPOUND-INTEREST FORMULA:

$$A = P\left(1 + \frac{r}{n}\right)^{nt}$$

In this formula, A is the future value of an investment, P is the initial deposit (or principal), r is the interest rate as a percentage, n is the number of times interest is compounded within a time period, or how often interest is applied to the account in a year (once per year, $n = 1$; monthly, $n = 12$; etc.), and t is the number of compounding cycles (usually years).

EXAMPLES

1) In the year 2000, the number of text messages sent in a small town totaled 124. If the number of text messages grew every year afterward by 124%, how many years would it take for the number of text messages to surpass 36,000?

Answer:

This is a growth problem that will require using the growth equation: $y = a(1 + r)^t$.

$y = 124(1 + 1.24)^t$
Write 124% as the decimal 1.24; the initial value is $a = 124$.

$y = 124(2.24)^t$
The question is asking when is $124(2.24)^x > 36,000$. One way to solve this is to graph $y_1 = 124(2.24)^x$ and $y_2 = 36,000$ on a calculator and look for when the first curve exceeds the second

curve. Find the intersection of these curves using the features of the calculator. This will give the exact time when the text messages exceed 36,000. This inequality can also be solved by solving the corresponding equations using logarithms, etc. However, it is rarely necessary to do this on a multiple-choice test. Often, the best approach is simply to plug the answer choices into the above equation to find which one works.

2) The half-life of a certain isotope is 5.5 years. If there were 20 grams of one such isotope left after 22 years, what was its original weight?

Answer:

$t = \frac{22}{5.5} = 4$	
$r = 0.5$	Identify the variables.
$a = ?$	
$20 = a(1 - 0.50)^4$	
$20 = a(0.5)^4$	
$20 = a\left(\frac{1}{2}\right)^4$	Plug these values into the decay formula and solve.
$20 = a\left(\frac{1}{16}\right)$	
$320 = a$	
The original weight is **320 grams**.	

3) If there were a glitch at a bank and a savings account accrued 5% interest five times per week, what would be the amount earned on a $50 deposit after twelve weeks?

Answer:

$r = 0.05$	
$n = 5$	Identify the variables.
$t = 12$	
$P = 50$	
$A = 50\left(1 + \frac{0.05}{5}\right)^{5(12)}$	Use the compound-interest formula, since this problem has many steps of growth within a time period.
$A = 50(1.01)^{60}$	
$A = 50(1.82) = 90.83$	
$90.83 - 50$	Subtract the original deposit to find the amount of interest earned.
= $40.83	

Polynomial Functions

A polynomial is any equation or expression with two or more terms with whole number exponents. All polynomials with only one variable are functions. The zeros, or roots, of a polynomial function are where the function equals zero and crosses the x-axis.

A linear function is a degree 1 polynomial and always has one zero. A quadratic function is a degree 2 polynomial and always has exactly two roots (including complex roots and counting repeated roots separately). This pattern is extended in the **Fundamental Theorem of Algebra**:

A polynomial function with degree $n > 0$ such as $f(x) = ax^n + bx^{n-1} + cx^{n-2} + \ldots + k$, has exactly n (real or complex) roots (some roots may be repeated). Simply stated, whatever the degree of the polynomial is, that is how many roots it will have.

Table 2.5. Zeros of Polynomial Functions

Polynomial Degree, N	Number and Possible Types of Zeros
1	1 real zero (guaranteed)
2	0, 1, or 2 real zeros possible 2 real **or** complex zeros (guaranteed)
3	1, 2, or 3 real zeros possible (there must be at least one real zero) Or 1 real zero (guaranteed) and 2 complex zeros (guaranteed)
4	0, 1, 2, 3, or 4 real zeros (possible) Or 2 real zeros and 2 complex zeros or 4 complex zeros
…	…

All the zeros of a polynomial satisfy the equation $f(x) = 0$. That is, if k is a zero of a polynomial, then plugging in $x = k$ into the polynomial results in 0. This also means that the polynomial is evenly divisible by the factor $(x - k)$.

All polynomials where n is an odd number will have at least one real zero or root. Complex zeros always come in pairs (specifically complex conjugate pairs).

EXAMPLE

Find the roots of the polynomial: $y = 3t^4 - 48$

Answer:

$y = 3t^4 - 48$	
$3(t^4 - 16) = 0$	Factor the polynomial. Remove the common factor of 3 from each term and make $y = 0$.

$3(t^2 - 4)(t^2 + 4) = 0$ $3(t + 2)(t - 2)(t^2 + 2) = 0$	Factor the difference of squares. $t^2 - 4$ is also a difference of squares.
$t + 2 = 0 \quad t - 2 = 0 \qquad t^2 + 2 = 0$ $t = -2 \qquad t = 2 \quad t^2 = -2$ $t = \pm\sqrt{-2} = \pm 2i$ This degree 4 polynomial has four roots, two real roots: **2 or −2**, and two complex roots: **2i or −2i**. The graph will have two x-intercepts at $(-2, 0)$ and $(2, 0)$.	Set each factor equal to zero. Solve each equation.

Modeling Relationships

Modeling relationships requires use of one of four of the function types examined above with an appropriate equation for a word problem or scenario.

Table 2.8. Function Types

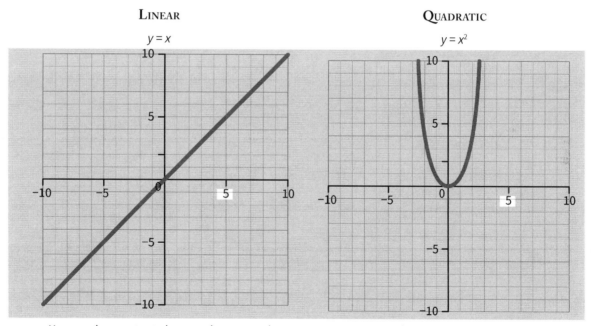

Key words: constant change, slope, equal   Key words: area, squared, parabola

GO ON

Table 2.8. Function Types (continued)

EXPONENTIAL

$y = a^x$

LOGARITHMIC

$y = \log(x)$

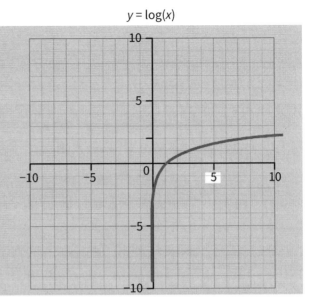

Key words: growth, decay, interest, double, triple, half-life

Key words: log-scale, base, log equations

Since exponential functions and log functions are inverses of each other, it will often be the case that exponential or log problems can be solved by either type of equation.

EXAMPLES

1) At a recent sporting event, there were 20,000 people in attendance. When it ended, people left the building at a rate of 1,000 people in the first minute, 1,000 more in the second minute, 1,000 in the third minute, and so on. What equation describes the behavior of attendees leaving the event for every minute after the event finished?

Answer:

The dependent variable is the number of attendees leaving the event (y). There is a constant change of 1,000 people per minute. Note that this is an additive pattern in the table: every increase of 1 in time results in a subtraction of the same value (1,000) in y. Because it is a constant rate of change, a linear model is required:

$y = 20,000 - 1,000x$

Here 20,000 is the y-intercept, and the rate of change, –1,000, is the slope.

To test this model, confirm that 18,000 attendees were left in the building after two minutes:

$y = 20,000 - 1,000(2) = 18,000$

The model is correct.

2) Consider the following sets of coordinate pairs of a function: {(-1, 0.4), (0, 1), (2, 6.25), and (3, 15.625)}. What kind of function does this represent?

Answer:

This function is not linear because there is not a constant change in the y value: the slope (rate of change) between (-1, 0.4), and (0, 1) is −0.6, whereas the slope between (0, 1) and (2, 6.25) is 2.625. There is also an x value that is negative, so it cannot be a logarithmic function (the domain of log functions is $x > 0$). Everything has been eliminated except quadratic and exponential. Graphing on the coordiante plane shows what looks like an exponential function.

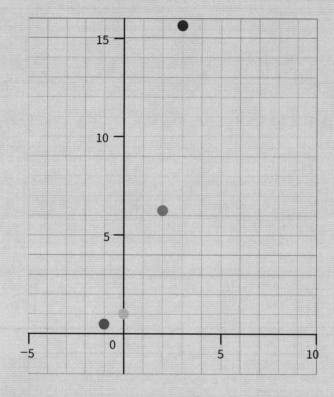

If it is exponential, then its equation is $y = ab^x$, where a is the y-intercept, so $a = 1$ in this case. The b is the growth or decay value. Plug in another point, such as (2, 6.25) to solve for b:

$y = ab^x$

$6.25 = (1)b^2$

$b = \sqrt{6.25} = 2.5$

The equation, then, is $y = 2.5^x$.

Check another point to confirm: Is $0.4 = 2.5^{-1}$? Since $2.5 = \frac{5}{2}$, and $\left(\frac{5}{2}\right)^{-1} = \frac{2}{5} = 0.4$, the equation works. The function is **exponential**.

Trigonometry

Trigonometry comes from the Greek words for *triangle* and *measuring*. Appropriately enough, trigonometry is used to find missing angles or side lengths in a triangle. Trigonometric questions often require use of algebraic skills with geometric concepts.

The Six Trigonometric Functions

There are six different trigonometric functions that are the foundations of trigonometry. They can be thought of as three pairs, as they are reciprocals of one another. All of these functions are ratios of the side lengths of a right triangle. The longest side of a right triangle (opposite the 90-degree angle) is called the **HYPOTENUSE**. The side directly opposite the angle being used is the **OPPOSITE**, and the side next to the angle is called the **ADJACENT** side.

Table 2.9. The Six Trigonometric Functions

Sine Function	Cosine Function	Tangent Function
$\sin\theta = \dfrac{\text{opposite}}{\text{hypotenuse}}$	$\cos\theta = \dfrac{\text{adjacent}}{\text{hypotenuse}}$	$\tan\theta = \dfrac{\text{opposite}}{\text{adjacent}}$
Cosecant Function	Secant Function	Cotangent Function
$\csc\theta = \dfrac{\text{hypotenuse}}{\text{opposite}}$	$\sec\theta = \dfrac{\text{hypotenuse}}{\text{adjacent}}$	$\cot\theta = \dfrac{\text{adjacent}}{\text{opposite}}$

There are a couple of special triangles that are used frequently and whose properties are worth memorizing. They are the 30° – 60° – 90° and the 45° – 45° – 90° triangles.

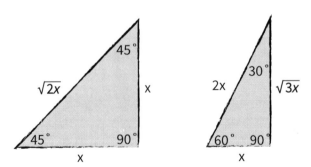

Figure 2.11. Special Right Triangles

For the 30° – 60° – 90° triangle, the side opposite the 30° angle (the shortest side) is always half the hypotenuse length, and the medium side (opposite the 60° angle) is $\sqrt{3}$ times the shortest side.

For the 45° – 45° – 90° triangle, two legs have the same length since two angles are equal (the triangle is isosceles), and the hypotenuse is always $\sqrt{2}$ times the length of a leg.

EXAMPLES

1) Find all six trigonometric ratios for the following triangle:

Answer:

The side directly opposite of θ is 15. The hypotenuse is the longest side with a length of 17. This leaves the 8 as the adjacent.

Sine Function	Cosine Function	Tangent Function
$\sin\theta = \frac{15}{17} = 0.88$	$\cos\theta = \frac{8}{17} = 0.47$	$\tan\theta = \frac{15}{8} = 1.88$
Cosecant Function	Secant Function	Cotangent Function
$\csc\theta = \frac{17}{15} = 1.13$	$\sec\theta = \frac{17}{8} = 2.13$	$\cot\theta = \frac{8}{15} = 0.53$

2) Find the missing length:

Answer:

Identify which side length is known, and which is being solved for in relation to the given angle. With respect to the 47-degree angle, the **h**ypotenuse is the unknown, and the known value is the **a**djacent. The trig function that uses adjacent and hypotenuse is cosine.

$\theta = 47$ degrees

$a = 3$ Identify the given parts of the triangle.

$h = x$

$\cos 47° = \frac{3}{x}$

$x(\cos 47°) = 3$ Plug these values into the equation for

$x = \frac{3}{\cos 47°}$ cosine and solve.

$= \textbf{4.41}$

3) Find the angle θ in degrees:

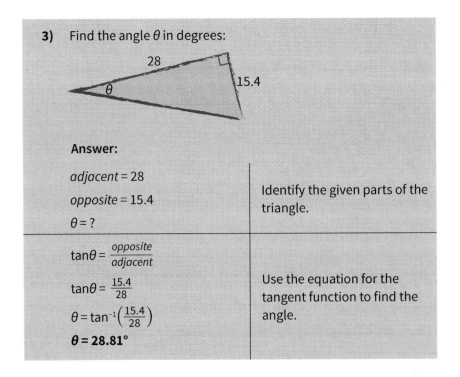

Answer:

adjacent = 28 *opposite* = 15.4 θ = ?	Identify the given parts of the triangle.
$\tan\theta = \dfrac{opposite}{adjacent}$ $\tan\theta = \dfrac{15.4}{28}$ $\theta = \tan^{-1}\left(\dfrac{15.4}{28}\right)$ **θ = 28.81°**	Use the equation for the tangent function to find the angle.

The Unit Circle

The **UNIT CIRCLE** is on the coordinate plane, with its center at the origin $(0,0)$ and a radius of 1. By using triangles within the unit circle (which will all have a hypotenuse of 1), the trigonometric ratios can be extended so that trigonometric functions of *any* angle may be evaluated.

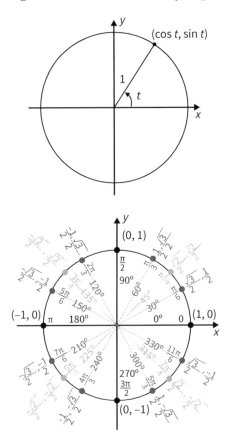

Figure 2.12. Unit Circle

In fact, each point (x, y) on the unit circle can be expressed as trig functions of the angle θ: $(x, y) = (\cos\theta, \sin\theta)$.

An angle in STANDARD POSITION in the plane has an initial (beginning) ray on the x-axis and a terminal (end) ray on the radius of the circle. Positive angles are measured in the counterclockwise direction, and negative angles are measured clockwise from the x-axis. One complete circle contains $360°$.

Another way to measure angles is with radians, which involves finding the length of the arc on the circle intercepted by the terminal ray of the angle. Since the circumference of the circle is $C = 2\pi r = 2\pi(1) = 2\pi$, the angle corresponding to one complete circle ($360°$) has a radian measure of 2π. Other angles can be expressed as fractions of 2π. For example, $90°$ is $\frac{1}{4}$ of a circle, so its radian measure is $\frac{1}{4}(2\pi) = \frac{\pi}{2}$. A $30°$ angle would be $\frac{30}{360}(2\pi)$ or $\frac{\pi}{6}$ radians. When the angle intersects the circle such that the arc length is 1, the corresponding angle is 1 radian. The angle in degrees at which this occurs is about $57.3°$, so 1 radian $\approx 57.3°$.

Angles can be converted between degrees and radians using these conversion factors:

$$\text{degrees} = \text{radians} \times \frac{180}{\pi} \qquad \text{radians} = \text{degrees} \times \frac{\pi}{180}$$

Any angle has an infinite number of COTERMINAL ANGLES associated with it. These are angles that share the same terminal ray. For example, $390°$ is coterminal with $30°$, because $390°$ is one complete revolution around the circle plus $30°$ more, so it lands on the same terminal ray. Another co-terminal angle to this angle would be $-330°$. To find co-terminal angles in degrees, simply add to or subtract $360°$ from the angle. In radians, add to or subtract 2π from the angle.

A calculator can be put in either radian or degree mode as appropriate for the given problem.

The unit circle diagram is made up of a number of specific sine and cosine coordinates for angles that are frequently used (often called special angles). Tangent on the unit circle is defined as the ratio of sine to cosine, $\tan\theta = \frac{\sin\theta}{\cos\theta}$.

Table 2.10. Special Angle Values in the First Quadrant

DEGREES	0	30	45	60	90
RADIANS	0	$\frac{\pi}{6}$	$\frac{\pi}{4}$	$\frac{\pi}{3}$	$\frac{\pi}{2}$
$\sin\theta$	0	$\frac{1}{2}$	$\frac{\sqrt{2}}{2}$	$\frac{\sqrt{3}}{2}$	1
$\cos\theta$	1	$\frac{\sqrt{3}}{2}$	$\frac{\sqrt{2}}{2}$	$\frac{1}{2}$	0
$\tan\theta$	0	$\frac{\sqrt{3}}{3}$	1	$\sqrt{3}$	undefined

When calculating trig functions of angles in other quadrants, make a sketch of the angle and drop a perpendicular altitude down to the nearest x-axis. This forms a triangle. The angle between the x-axis and the terminal ray is called the REFERENCE ANGLE. It will always be an angle between 0 and $\frac{\pi}{2}$ (or 0 and 90°). If it is one of the special angles, either label the sides of the triangles using the special triangle rules, or use the table above to find the value. In either case, care must be given to the *sign* of the value. As the terminal ray travels into quadrants 2, 3, and 4, the signs of the x- and y-coordinates are sometimes negative, so the corresponding trig functions will also be negative. This diagram summarizes where each trig function is *positive* (where it is not positive, it is negative!).

Q 2 sinθ and cscθ +	Q 1 ALL trig functions +
Q 3 tanθ and cotθ +	Q 4 cosθ and secθ +

Figure 2.18. Trigonometric Signs by Quadrant

EXAMPLES

1) Find $\sin\frac{\pi}{2}$.

Answer:

To make use of a graphing calculator's trigonometric function, make sure it is in radian mode and type in: $\sin\frac{\pi}{2}$, which returns a value of 1. To understand *why* this is true, locate the angle $\frac{\pi}{2}$ on the unit circle. The $\sin\frac{\pi}{2}$ is the y-coordinate of the intersection of the terminal ray of angle $\frac{\pi}{2}$ with the unit circle, which is 1 because the ray intersects the circle at point $(0, 1)$.

2) Find $\csc\left(\frac{7\pi}{4}\right)$.

Answer:

$\csc\frac{7\pi}{4} = \frac{1}{\sin\frac{7\pi}{4}}$	Rewrite the expression using the reciprocal identity.
$\sin\frac{7\pi}{4} = \frac{1}{\sqrt{2}}$	Find $\frac{7\pi}{4}$ on the unit circle.
$\csc\frac{7\pi}{4} = \frac{1}{\sin\frac{7\pi}{4}} = \frac{1}{\frac{1}{\sqrt{2}}} = \sqrt{2}$	Convert sine into cosecant.

Non-Right Triangles

Trigonometry is usually associated with right triangles. However, trigonometric functions can be used to solve for a missing side or angle in an oblique triangle (a triangle without any 90° angles). To solve an oblique triangle, either two sides and one angle, two angles and any one side, or all three sides must be known.

THE LAW OF SINES is based on the proportionality between the sine of angles in a triangle and the sides of the triangle. It states, based on a triangle ABC with angles A, B, and C and corresponding sides a, b, c (a is the side opposite angle A, etc.):

$$\frac{a}{\sin A} = \frac{b}{\sin B} = \frac{c}{\sin C}$$

While all three proportionalities always hold, in practice only two of the three ratios are used at one time.

THE LAW OF COSINES can be used when three sides are known, or when two sides and the included angle between those two sides are known. The law of cosines is based on Pythagorean identities:

$$c^2 = a^2 + b^2 - 2ab\cos(C)$$

$$b^2 = a^2 + c^2 - 2ac\cos(B)$$

$$a^2 = b^2 + c^2 - 2bc\cos(A)$$

EXAMPLES

1) Find the degree measure of C in the following triangle, where c = 12, b = 7, and a = 8.

Answer:

Since three sides are given, use the law of cosines:

$12^2 = 8^2 + 7^2 - 2(8)(7)\cos C$	Begin with "12^2 = " because 12 is opposite the angle sought.
$144 = 64 + 49 - 112\cos C$	Simplify squares and products.
$31 = -112\cos C$	Subtract 64 and 49 from both sides.
$\cos C = \frac{31}{-112}$	Divide both sides by –112.
$= \cos^{-1}\left(\frac{31}{112}\right)$ $= \mathbf{106.1°}$	Use inverse cosine to find the angle.

2) If there is a triangle where $a = 110$, $c = 40$, and the measure of angle $A = 110°$, what is the measure of angle C?

Answer:

Because an angle and the side opposite is known, and the side opposite the unknown angle is known, use the law of sines for this triangle:

$a = 110$	
$A = 110°$	Identify the parts of the triangle given.
$c = 40$	
$C = ?$	
$\frac{40}{\sin C} = \frac{110}{\sin 110}$	
$40(\sin 110) = 110 \sin C$	Plug these values into the law of
$\frac{37.6}{110} = \sin C$	sines and solve for angle C.
$.34 = \sin C$	
$C = \sin^{-1}(.34)$	Plug these values into the law of sines and solve for angle C
$= \mathbf{20°}$	(continued).

Test Your Skills

1) Which of the following is equivalent to $54z^4 + 18z^3 + 3z + 3$?

   A. $18z^4 + 6z^3 + z + 1$

   B. $3z(18z^3 + 6z^2 + 1)$

   C. $72z^7 + 3z$

   D. $3(18z^4 + 6z^3 + z + 1)$

2) What is the x-intercept of the given equation?

   $10x + 10y = 10$

   A. $(1, 0)$

   B. $(0, 1)$

   C. $(0, 0)$

   D. $(1, 1)$

3) Which of the following is a solution to the inequality $2x + y \leq -10$?

   A. $(0, 0)$

   B. $(10, 2)$

   C. $(10, 10)$

   D. $(-10, -10)$

4) What is the maximum value of the function $f(x) = 3\sin(x - 2) + 1$?

   A. 1

   B. 3

   C. 4

   D. 7

5) Which of the following are the vertical asymptotes of the given function?

   $f(x) = \frac{x^3 - 16x}{-4x^2 + 4x + 24}$

   A. $x = -4$ and $x = 4$

   B. $x = -3$ and $x = 2$

   C. $x = -2$ and $x = 3$

   D. $x = 0$ and $x = 4$

6) Find $f(x) = (j \circ t)(x)$ if $j(x) = \frac{1}{3}x - 2$ and $t(x) = \frac{1}{2}x - 3$.

   A. $f(x) = \frac{1}{6}x^2 + 6$

   B. $f(x) = \frac{1}{6}x^2 - 5x + 6$

   C. $f(x) = \frac{1}{6}x - 4$

   D. $f(x) = \frac{1}{6}x - 3$

7) If the smallest angle in a non-right triangle is 20° and the shortest side is 14, what is the length of the largest side if the largest angle is 100°?

   A. 12.78

   B. 34.31

   C. 40.31

   D. 127.81

8) Which expression is equivalent to $5^2 \times (-5)^{-2} - (2 + 3)^{-1}$?

   A. 0

   B. 1

   C. $\frac{5}{4}$

   D. $\frac{4}{5}$

9) If $16^{x + 10} = 8^{3x}$, what is the value of x?

   Write in the answer: _____

10) What is the greatest number of complex roots a 17th degree polynomial can have?

   Write in the answer: _____

Answer Key

1) **D.** Factor the expression using the greatest common factor of 3.

$54z^4 + 18z^3 + 3z + 3 =$

$$\mathbf{3(18z^4 + 6z^3 + z + 1)}$$

2) **A.** Plug 0 in for y and solve for x.

$10x + 10y = 10$

$10x + 10(0) = 10$

$x = 1$

The x-intercept is at **$(1, 0)$**.

3) **D.** Plug in each set of values and determine if the inequality is true.

$2(0) + 0 \leq -10$ FALSE

$2(10) + 2 \leq -10$ FALSE

$2(10) + 10 \leq -10$ FALSE

$2(-10) + (-10) \leq -10$ TRUE

4) **C.** This sine function has an amplitude of 3 and has been shifted up 1, so it has a maximum value of **4**.

5) **C.** Make sure there are no factors that cancel, and then set the denominator equal to 0.

$$\frac{x^3 - 16x}{-4x^2 + 4x + 24} = \frac{x(x^2 - 16)}{-4(x^2 - x - 6)}$$

$$= \frac{x(x+4)(x-4)}{-4(x-3)(x+2)}$$

The graph has no holes.

$-4(x - 3)(x + 2) = 0$

$\boldsymbol{x = 3}$ and $\boldsymbol{x = -2}$

6) **D.** To find the compound function, substitute $t(x)$ for x in $j(x)$.

$(j \circ t)(x) = \frac{1}{3}\left(\frac{1}{2}x - 3\right) - 2 = \mathbf{\frac{1}{6}x - 3}$

7) **C.** Use the law of sines.

$$\frac{\sin 20°}{14} = \frac{\sin 100°}{x}$$

$$x = \frac{14(\sin 100°)}{\sin 20°}$$

$\boldsymbol{x = 40.31}$

8) **D.** Simplify using PEMDAS.

$5^2 \times (-5)^{-2} - 5^{-1}$

$= 25 \times \frac{1}{25} - \frac{1}{5}$

$= 1 - \frac{1}{5}$

$= \mathbf{\frac{4}{5}}$

9) Rewrite the bases so they are the same, then set the exponents equal and solve.

$16^{x+10} = 8^{3x}$

$(2^4)^{x+10} = (2^3)^{3x}$

$2^{4x+40} = 2^{9x}$

$4x + 40 = 9x$

$\boldsymbol{x = 8}$

10) Complex solutions always come in pairs. Therefore, the number of possible complex solutions is the greatest *even* number equal to or less than the power of the polynomial. A 17th degree polynomial can have at most **16** complex roots.

three

GEOMETRY

Geometry is the study of shapes, angles, volumes, areas, lines, points, and the relationships among them. It is normally approached as an axiomatic system; that is, a small number of entities are taken for granted as true, and everything else is derived logically from them.

Equality, Congruence, and Similarity

When discussing shapes in geometry, the term **CONGRUENT** is used to mean that two shapes have the same shape and size (but not necessarily the same orientation or location). This concept is slightly different from equality, which is used in geometry to describe numerical values. For example, if the length of two lines are equal, the two lines themselves are called congruent. Congruence is written using the symbol ≅. On figures, congruent parts are denoted with hash marks.

Shapes which are **SIMILAR** have the same shape but the not the same size, meaning their corresponding angles are the same but their lengths are not. For two shapes to be similar, the ratio of their corresponding sides must be a constant (usually written as k). Similarity is described using the symbol ~.

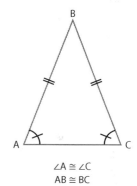

$$\angle A \cong \angle C$$
$$AB \cong BC$$

Figure 3.1. Congruent Parts of a Triangle

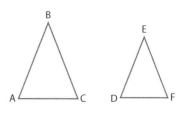

$$ABC \sim DEF$$
$$\frac{AB}{DE} = \frac{BC}{EF} = \frac{AC}{DF}$$

Figure 3.2. Similar Triangles

Properties of Shapes

Basic Definitions

The basic figures from which many other geometric shapes are built are points, lines, and planes. A **POINT** is a location in a plane. It has no size or shape, but is represented by a dot. It is labeled using a capital letter.

A LINE is a one-dimensional collection of points that extends infinitely in both directions. At least two points are needed to define a line, and any points that lie on the same line are COLINEAR. Lines are represented by two points, such as *A* and *B*, and the line symbol: ($\overleftrightarrow{AB}$). Two lines on the same plane will intersect unless they are PARALLEL, meaning they have the same slope. Lines that intersect at a 90 degree angle are PERPENDICULAR.

A LINE SEGMENT has two endpoints and a finite length. The length of a segment, called the measure of the segment, is the distance from *A* to *B*. A line segment is a subset of a line, and is also denoted with two points, but with a segment symbol: ($\overline{AB}$). The MIDPOINT of a line segment is the point at which the segment is divided into two equal parts. A line, segment, or plane that passes through the midpoint of a segment is called a BISECTOR of the segment, since it cuts the segment into two equal segments.

A RAY has one endpoint and extends indefinitely in one direction. It is defined by its endpoint, followed by any other point on the ray: $\overrightarrow{AB}$. It is important that the first letter represents the endpoint. A ray is sometimes called a half line.

Table 3.1. Basic Geometric Figures

TERM	DIMENSIONS	GRAPHIC	SYMBOL
point	zero		·*A*
line segment	one		$\overline{AB}$
ray	one		$\overrightarrow{AB}$
line	one		$\overleftrightarrow{AB}$
plane	two		Plane *M*

A PLANE is a flat sheet that extends indefinitely in two directions (like an infinite sheet of paper). A plane is a two-dimensional (2D) figure. A plane can always be defined through any three noncollinear points in three-dimensional (3D) space. A plane is named using any three points that are in the plane (for example, plane *ABC*). Any points lying in the same plane are said to be COPLANAR. When two planes intersect, the intersection is a line.

EXAMPLE

Which points and lines are not contained in plane *M* in the diagram below?

Answer:

Points *A* and *B* and line *D* are all on plane *M*. Point *C* is above the plane, and line *E* cuts through the plane and thus does not lie on plane *M*. The point at which line *E* intersects plane *M* is on plane *M* but the line as a whole is not.

Angles

ANGLES are formed when two rays share a common endpoint. They are named using three letters, with the vertex point in the middle (for example ∠*ABC*, where *B* is the vertex). They can also be labeled with a number or named by their vertex alone (if it is clear to do so). Angles are also classified based on their angle measure. A **RIGHT ANGLE** has a measure of exactly 90°. **ACUTE ANGLES** have measures that are less than 90°, and **OBTUSE ANGLES** have measures that are greater than 90°.

Angles can be measured in degrees or radian. Use the conversion factor
1 rad = 57.3 degrees
to convert between them.

Any two angles that add to make 90° are called **COMPLEMENTARY ANGLES**. A 30° angle would be complementary to a 60° angle. **SUPPLEMENTARY ANGLES** add up to 180°. A supplementary angle to a 60° angle would be a 120° angle; likewise, 60° is the **SUPPLEMENT** of 120°. Angles that are next to each other and share a common ray are called **ADJACENT ANGLES**. Angles that are adjacent and supplementary are called a **LINEAR PAIR** of angles. Their nonshared rays form a line (thus the *linear* pair). Note that angles that are supplementary do not need to be adjacent; their measures simply need to add to 180°.

VERTICAL ANGLES are formed when two lines intersect. Four angles will be formed; the vertex of each angle is at the intersection point of the lines. The vertical angles across from each other will be equal in measure. The angles adjacent to each other will be linear pairs and therefore supplementary.

A ray, line, or segment that divides an angle into two equal angles is called an **ANGLE BISECTOR**.

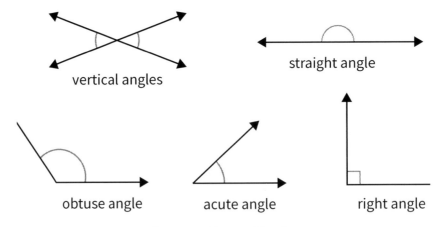

Figure 3.3. Types of Angles

vertical angles

straight angle

obtuse angle

acute angle

right angle

EXAMPLES

1) How many linear pairs of angles are there in the following figure?

Answers:

Any two adjacent angles that are supplementary are linear pairs, so there are 16 linear pairs in the figure ($\angle 1$ and $\angle 5$, $\angle 2$ and $\angle 6$, $\angle 5$ and $\angle 6$, $\angle 2$ and $\angle 1$, and so on).

2) If angles M and N are supplementary and $\angle M$ is 30° less than twice $\angle N$, what is the degree measurement of each angle?

Answer:

$\angle M + \angle N = 180°$

$\angle M = 2\angle N - 30°$

Set up a system of equations.

$\angle M + \angle N = 180°$	
$(2\angle N - 30°) + \angle N = 180°$	
$3\angle N - 30° = 180°$	Use substitution to solve for $\angle N$.
$3\angle N = 210°$	
$\angle N = 70°$	
$\angle M + \angle N = 180°$	
$\angle M + 70° = 180°$	Solve for $\angle M$ using the original equation.
$\angle M = \mathbf{110°}$	

Circles

A **CIRCLE** is the set of all the points in a plane that are the same distance from a fixed point called the **CENTER**. The distance from the center to any point on the circle is the **RADIUS** of the circle. The distance around the circle (the perimeter) is called the **CIRCUMFERENCE**.

The ratio of a circle's circumference to its diameter is a constant value called pi (π), an irrational number which is commonly rounded to 3.14. The formula to find a circle's circumference is $C = 2\pi r$. The formula to find the enclosed area of a circle is $A = \pi r^2$.

Circles have a number of unique parts and properties:

♦ The **DIAMETER** is the largest measurement across a circle. It passes through the circle's center, extending from one side of the circle to the other. The measure of the diameter is twice the measure of the radius.

♦ A line that cuts across a circle and touches it twice is called a **SECANT** line. The part of a secant line that lies within a circle is called a **CHORD**. Two chords within a circle are of equal length if they are the same distance from the center.

♦ A line that touches a circle or any curve at one point is **TANGENT** to the circle or the curve. These lines are always exterior to the circle. A line tangent to a circle and a radius drawn to the point of tangency meet at a right angle (90°).

♦ An **ARC** is any portion of a circle between two points on the circle. The **MEASURE** of an arc is in degrees, whereas the **LENGTH OF THE ARC** will be in linear measurement (such as centimeters or inches). A **MINOR ARC** is the small arc between the two points (it measures less than 180°), whereas a **MAJOR ARC** is the large arc between the two points (it measures greater than 180°).

♦ An angle with its vertex at the center of a circle is called a **CENTRAL ANGLE**. For a central angle, the measure of the arc intercepted by the sides of the angle (in degrees) is the same as the measure of the angle.

Trying to square a circle means attempting to create a square that has the same area as a circle. Because the area of a circle depends on π, which is an irrational number, this task is impossible. The phrase is often used to describe trying to do something that can't be done.

- A **SECTOR** is the part of a circle *and* its interior that is inside the rays of a central angle (its shape is like a slice of pie).

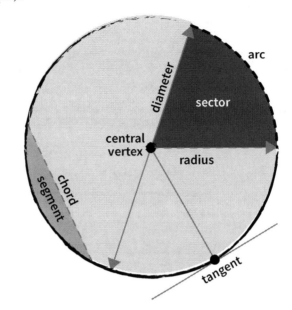

Figure 3.4. Parts of a Circle

	Area of Sector	Length of an Arc
Degrees	$A = \frac{\theta}{360°} \times \pi r^2$	$s = \frac{\theta}{360°} \times 2\pi r$
Radians	$A = \frac{1}{2}\pi^2\theta$	$s = r\theta$

- An **INSCRIBED ANGLE** has a vertex on the circle and is formed by two chords that share that vertex point. The angle measure of an inscribed angle is one-half the angle measure of the central angle with the same endpoints on the circle.

- A **CIRCUMSCRIBED ANGLE** has rays tangent to the circle. The angle lies outside of the circle.

- Any angle outside the circle, whether formed by two tangent lines, two secant lines, or a tangent line and a secant line, is equal to half the difference of the intercepted arcs.

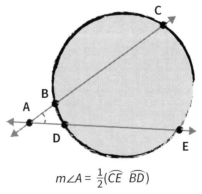

$$m\angle A = \tfrac{1}{2}(\widehat{CE}\ \widehat{BD})$$

Figure 3.5. Angles Outside a Circle

◆ Angles are formed within a circle when two chords intersect in the circle. The measure of the smaller angle formed is half the sum of the two smaller arc measures (in degrees). Likewise, the larger angle is half the sum of the two larger arc measures.

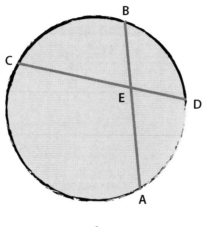

$$m\angle E = \tfrac{1}{2}(\widehat{AC} + \widehat{BD})$$

Figure 3.6. Intersecting Chords

◆ If a chord intersects a line tangent to the circle, the angle formed by this intersection measures one half the measurement of the intercepted arc (in degrees).

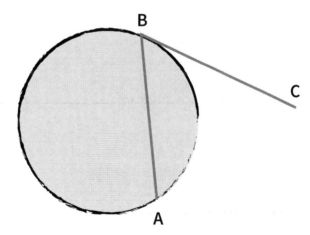

$$m\angle ABC = \tfrac{1}{2}m\widehat{AB}$$

Figure 3.7. Intersecting Chord and Tangent

GO ON

EXAMPLES

1) Find the area of the sector *NHS* of the circle below with center at *H*:

Answer:

$r = 4$ $\angle NHS = 90°$	Identify the important parts of the circle.
$A = \dfrac{\theta}{360°} \times \pi r^2$ $= \dfrac{90}{360} \times \pi(4)^2$	Plug these values into the formula for the area of a sector.
$= \dfrac{1}{4} \times 16\pi$ $= \mathbf{4\pi}$	Plug these values into the formula for the area of a sector (continued).

2) In the circle below with center *O*, the minor arc *ACB* measures 5 feet. What is the measurement of *m∠AOB*?

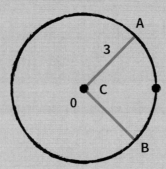

Answer:

$r = 3$ length of $\overline{ACB} = 5$	Identify the important parts of the circle.
$s = \dfrac{\theta}{360°} \times 2\pi r$ $5 = \dfrac{\theta}{360°} \times 2\pi(3)$ $\dfrac{5}{6\pi} = \dfrac{\theta}{360°}$ $\theta = 95.5°$ $\boldsymbol{m\angle AOB = 95.5°}$	Plug these values into the formula for the length of an arc and solve for θ.

Triangles

Much of geometry is concerned with triangles as they are commonly used shapes. A good understanding of triangles allows decomposition of other shapes (specifically polygons) into triangles for study.

Triangles have three sides, and the three interior angles always sum to 180°. The formula for the area of a triangle is $A = \frac{1}{2}bh$ or one-half the product of the base and height (or altitude) of the triangle.

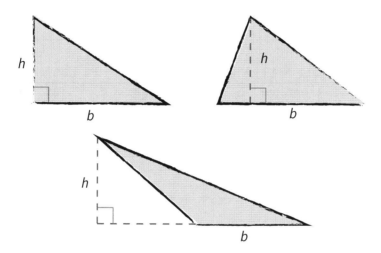

Figure 3.8. Finding the Base and Height of Triangles

Some important segments in a triangle include the angle bisector, the altitude, and the median. The ANGLE BISECTOR extends from the side opposite an angle to bisect that angle. The ALTITUDE is the shortest distance from a vertex of the triangle to the line containing the base side opposite that vertex. It is perpendicular to that line and can occur on the outside of the triangle. The MEDIAN extends from an angle to bisect the opposite side.

Angle Bisector
Divides angle in half

Altitude
Shortest distance to side

Median
Divides opposite side in half

Figure 3.9. Important Segments in a Triangle

Triangles have two "centers." The ORTHOCENTER is formed by the intersection of a triangle's three altitudes. The CENTROID is where a triangle's three medians meet.

Triangles can be classified in two ways: by sides and by angles.

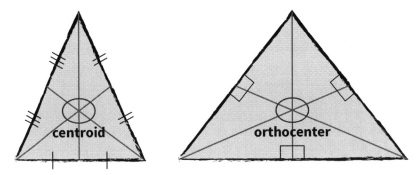

Figure 3.10. Centroid and Orthocenter of a Triangle

A SCALENE TRIANGLE has no equal sides or angles. An ISOSCELES TRIANGLE has two equal sides and two equal angles, often called BASE ANGLES. In an EQUILATERAL TRIANGLE, all three sides are equal as are all three angles. Moreover, because the sum of the angles of a triangle is always 180°, each angle of an equilateral triangle must be 60°.

A RIGHT TRIANGLE has one right angle (90°) and two acute angles. An ACUTE TRIANGLE has three acute angles (all angles are less than 90°). An OBTUSE TRIANGLE has one obtuse angle (more than 90°) and two acute angles.

Triangles Based on Sides

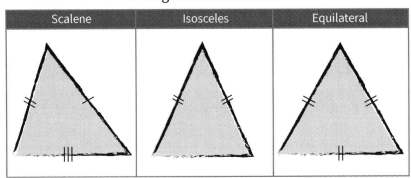

Triangles Based on Angles

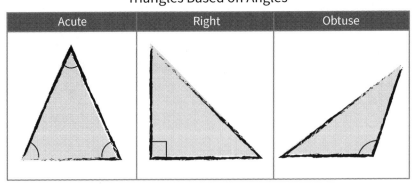

Figure 3.11. Types of Triangles

Trigonometric functions can be employed to find missing sides and angles of a triangle.

For any triangle, the side opposite the largest angle will have the longest length, while the side opposite the smallest angle will have the shortest length. The TRIANGLE INEQUALITY THEOREM states that the sum of any two sides of a triangle must be greater than the third side. If this inequality does not hold, then a triangle cannot be formed. A consequence of this theorem is the THIRD-SIDE RULE: if b and c are two sides of a triangle, then the measure of the third side a must be between the sum of the other two sides and the difference of the other two sides: $c - b < a < c + b$.

Solving for missing angles or sides of a triangle is a common type of triangle problem. Often a right triangle will come up on its own or within another triangle. The relationship among a right triangle's sides is known as the PYTHAGOREAN THEOREM: $a^2 + b^2 = c^2$, where c is the hypotenuse and is across from the 90° angle. Right triangles with angle measurements of 90° – 45° – 45° and 90° – 60° – 30° are known as "special" right triangles and have specific relationships between their sides and angles.

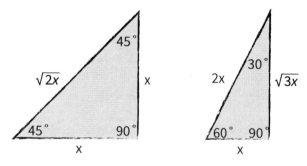

Figure 3.12. Special Right Triangles

EXAMPLES

1) What are the minimum and maximum values of x to the nearest hundredth?

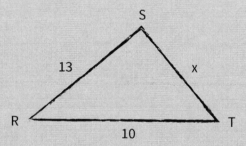

Answers:

The sum of two sides is 23 and their difference is 3. To connect the two other sides and enclose a space, x must be less than the sum and greater than the difference (that is, $3 < x < 23$). Therefore, **x's minimum value to the nearest hundredth is 3.01 and its maximum value is 22.99.**

2) Examine and classify each of the following triangles:

1.

2.

3.

4.

Answers:

Triangle 1 is an equilateral triangle (all 3 sides are equal, and all 3 angles are equal)

Triangle 2 is a scalene, right triangle (all 3 sides are different, and there is a 90° angle)

Triangle 3 is an isosceles triangle (there are 2 equal sides and, consequently, 2 equal angles)

Triangle 4 is a right, isosceles triangle (there are 2 equal sides and a 90° angle)

3) Given the diagram, if $XZ = 100$, $WZ = 80$, and $XU = 70$, then $WY = ?$

Answer:

$WZ = b_1 = 80$

$XU = h_1 = 70$

$XZ = b_2 = 100$

$WY = h_2 = ?$

$A = \frac{1}{2}bh$

$A_1 = \frac{1}{2}(80)(70) = 2800$

$A_2 = \frac{1}{2}(100)(h_2)$

$2800 = \frac{1}{2}(100)(h_2)$

$h_2 = 56$

WY = 56

The given values can be used to write two equation for the area of $\triangle WXZ$ with two sets of bases and heights.

Set the two equations equal to each other and solve for *WY*.

Quadrilaterals

All closed, four-sided shapes are QUADRILATERALS. The sum of all internal angles in a quadrilateral is always 360°. (Think of drawing a diagonal to create two triangles. Since each triangle contains 180°, two triangles, and therefore the quadrilateral, must contain 360°.) The AREA OF ANY QUADRILATERAL is $A = bh$, where *b* is the base and *h* is the height (or altitude).

A PARALLELOGRAM is a quadrilateral with two pairs of parallel sides. A rectangle is a parallelogram with two pairs of equal sides and four right angles. A KITE also has two pairs of equal sides, but its equal sides are consecutive. Both a SQUARE and a RHOMBUS have four equal sides. A square has four right angles, while a rhombus has a pair of acute opposite angles and a pair of obtuse opposite angles. A TRAPEZOID has exactly one pair of parallel sides.

All squares are rectangles and all rectangles are parallelograms; however, not all parallelograms are rectangles and not all rectangles are squares.

Table 3.2 Properties of Parallelograms

TERM	SHAPE	PROPERTIES
Parallelogram		Opposite sides are parallel. Consecutive angles are supplementary. Opposite angles are equal. Opposite sides are equal. Diagonals bisect each other.
Rectangle		All parallelogram properties hold. Diagonals are congruent *and* bisect each other. All angles are right angles.
Square		All rectangle properties hold. All four sides are equal. Diagonals bisect angles. Diagonals intersect at right angles and bisect each other.

Table 3.2 Properties of Parallelograms (continued)

Term	Shape	Properties
Kite		One pair of opposite angles is equal. Two pairs of consecutive sides are equal. Diagonals meet at right angles.
Rhombus		All four sides are equal. Diagonals bisect angles. Diagonals intersect at right angles and bisect each other.
Trapezoid		One pair of sides is parallel. Bases have different lengths. Isosceles trapezoids have a pair of equal sides (and base angles).

EXAMPLES

1) In parallelogram *ABCD*, the measure of angle *m* is is $m° = 260°$. What is the measure of $n°$?

Answers:

$260° + m\angle C = 360°$ $m\angle C = 100°$	Find $\angle C$ using the fact that the sum of $\angle C$ and *m* is 360°.
$m\angle C + m\angle D = 180°$ $100° + m\angle D = 180°$ $m\angle D = 80°$	Solve for $\angle D$ using the fact that consecutive interior angles in a quadrilateral are supplementary.
$m\angle D + n = 360°$ **$n = 280°$**	Solve for *n* by subtracting $m\angle D$ from 360°.

2) A rectangular section of a football field has dimensions of *x* and *y* and an area of 1000 square feet. Three additional lines drawn vertically divide the section into four smaller rectangular areas as seen in the diagram below. If all the lines

shown need to be painted, calculate the total number of linear feet, in terms of x, to be painted.

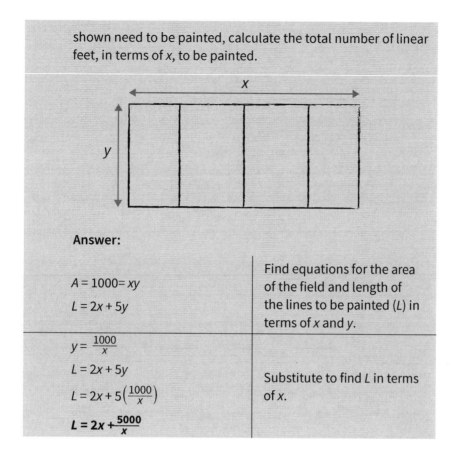

Answer:

$A = 1000 = xy$ $L = 2x + 5y$	Find equations for the area of the field and length of the lines to be painted (L) in terms of x and y.
$y = \frac{1000}{x}$ $L = 2x + 5y$ $L = 2x + 5\left(\frac{1000}{x}\right)$ $L = 2x + \frac{5000}{x}$	Substitute to find L in terms of x.

Polygons

Any closed shape made up of three or more line segments is a polygon. In addition to triangles and quadrilaterals, HEXAGONS and OCTAGONS are two common polygons.

Octagon
an eight-sided polygon

Hexagon
a six-sided polygon

Figure 3.13. Common Polygons

The two polygons depicted above are REGULAR POLYGONS, meaning that they are equilateral (all sides having equal lengths) and equiangular (all angles having equal measurements). Angles inside a polygon are INTERIOR ANGLES, whereas those formed by one side of the polygon and a line extending outside the polygon are EXTERIOR ANGLES:

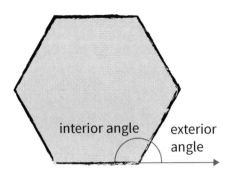

Figure 3.14 Interior and Exterior Angles

Breaking an irregular polygon down into triangles and quadrilaterals helps in finding its area.

The sum of the all the exterior angles of a polygon is always 360°. Dividing 360° by the number of a polygon's sides finds the measure of the polygon's exterior angles.

To determine the sum of a polygon's interior angles, choose one vertex and draw diagonals from that vertex to each of the other vertices, decomposing the polygon into multiple triangles. For example, an octagon has six triangles within it, and therefore the sum of the interior angles is $6 \times 180° = 1080°$. In general, the formula for finding the sum of the angles in a polygon is *sum of angles* $= (n - 2) \times 180°$, where n is the number of sides of the polygon.

To find the measure of a single interior angle, simply divide the sum of the interior angles by the number of angles (which is the same as the number of sides). So, in the octagon example, each angle is $\frac{1080}{8} = 135°$.

In general, the formula to find the measure of a regular polygon's interior angles is: *interior angle* $= \frac{(n - 2)}{n} \times 180°$ where n is the number of sides of the polygon.

To find the area of a polygon, it is helpful to know the perimeter of the polygon (p), and the **APOTHEM** (a). The apothem is the shortest (perpendicular) distance from the polygon's center to one of the sides of the polygon. The formula for the area is: *area* $= \frac{ap}{2}$.

Finally, there is no universal way to find the perimeter of a polygon (when the side length is not given). Often, breaking the polygon down into triangles and adding the base of each triangle all the way around the polygon is the easiest way to calculate the perimeter.

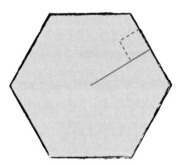

Figure 3.15. Apothem in a Hexagon

EXAMPLES

1) What is the measure of an exterior angle and an interior angle of a regular 400-gon?

Answer:

The sum of the exterior angles is 360°. Dividing this sum by 400 gives $\frac{360°}{400} = $ **0.9°**. Since an interior angle is supplementary to an exterior angle, all the interior angles have measure 180 − 0.9 = **179.1°**. Alternately, using the formula for calculating the interior angle gives the same result:

$$interior\ angle = \frac{400 - 2}{400} \times 180° = 179.1°$$

2) The circle and hexagon below both share center point T. The hexagon is entirely inscribed in the circle. The circle's radius is 5. What is the area of the shaded area?

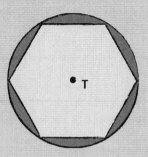

Answer:

$A_c = \pi r^2$ $= \pi(5)^2$ $= 25\pi$	The area of the shaded region will be the area of the circle minus the area of the hexagon. Use the radius to find the area of the circle.
  $a = 2.5\sqrt{3}$ $A_H = \frac{ap}{2}$ $= \frac{(2.5\sqrt{3})(30)}{2}$ $= 64.95$	To find the area of the hexagon, draw a right triangle from the vertex, and use special right triangles to find the hexagon's apothem. Then, use the apothem to calculate the area.
$= A_c - A_H$ $= 25\pi - 2.5\sqrt{3}$ ≈ 13.59	Subtract the area of the hexagon from the circle to find the area of the shaded region.

Three-Dimensional Shapes

Properties of Three-Dimensional Shapes

THREE-DIMENSIONAL SHAPES have depth in addition to width and length. VOLUME is expressed as the number of cubic units any solid can hold—that is, what it takes to fill it up. SURFACE AREA is the sum of the areas of the two-dimensional figures that are found on its surface.

Some three-dimensional shapes also have a unique property called a slant height (ℓ), which is the distance from the base to the apex along a lateral face.

Table 3.3 Three-Dimensional Shapes and Formulas

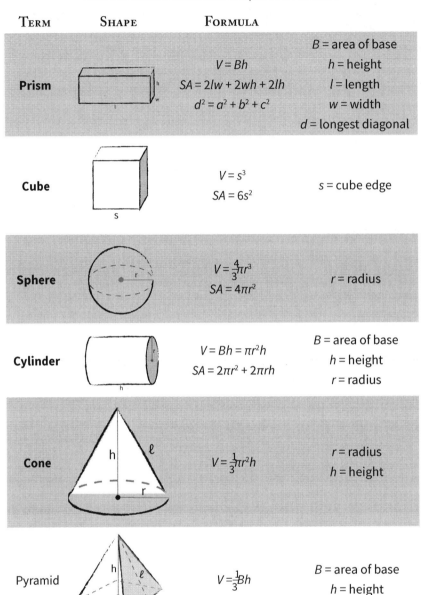

Term	Shape	Formula	
Prism		$V = Bh$ $SA = 2lw + 2wh + 2lh$ $d^2 = a^2 + b^2 + c^2$	B = area of base h = height l = length w = width d = longest diagonal
Cube		$V = s^3$ $SA = 6s^2$	s = cube edge
Sphere		$V = \frac{4}{3}\pi r^3$ $SA = 4\pi r^2$	r = radius
Cylinder		$V = Bh = \pi r^2 h$ $SA = 2\pi r^2 + 2\pi rh$	B = area of base h = height r = radius
Cone		$V = \frac{1}{3}\pi r^2 h$	r = radius h = height
Pyramid		$V = \frac{1}{3}Bh$	B = area of base h = height

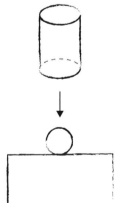

Figure 3.16. Net of a Cylinder

Finding the surface area of a three-dimensional solid can be made easier by using a NET. This two-dimensional "flattened" version of a three-dimensional shape shows the component parts that comprise the surface of the solid.

EXAMPLES

1) A sphere has a radius z. If that radius is increased by t, by how much is the surface area increased? Write the answer in terms of z and t.

Answer:

$SA_1 = 4\pi z^2$	Write the equation for the area of the original sphere.
$SA_2 = 4\pi(z + t)^2$ $= 4\pi(z^2 + 2zt + t^2)$ $= 4\pi z^2 + 8\pi zt + 4\pi t^2$	Write the equation for the area of the new sphere.
$A_2 - A_1 = 4\pi z^2 + 8\pi zt + 4\pi t^2$ $- 4\pi z^2$ $\mathbf{= 4\pi t^2 + 8\pi zt}$	To find the difference between the two, subtract the original from the increased surface area:

2) A cube with volume 27 cubic meters is inscribed within a sphere such that all of the cube's vertices touch the sphere. What is the length of the sphere's radius?

Answer:

Since the cube's volume is 27, each side length is equal to $\sqrt[3]{27} =$ 3. The long diagonal distance from one of the cube's vertices to its opposite vertex will provide the sphere's diameter:

$d = \sqrt{3^2 + 3^2 + 3^2} = \sqrt{27} = 5.2$

Half of this length is the radius, which is **2.6 meters**.

Congruence and Similarity in Three-Dimensional Shapes

Three-dimensional shapes may also be congruent if they are the same size and shape, or similar if their corresponding parts are proportional. For example, a pair of cones is similar if the ratios of the cones' radii and heights are proportional. For rectangular prisms, all three dimensions must be proportional for the prisms to be similar. If two shapes are similar, their corresponding areas and volumes will also be proportional. If the constant of proportionality of the linear measurements of a 3D shape is k, the constant of proportionality between the areas will be k^2, and the constant of proportionality between the volumes will be k^3.

All spheres are similar as a dilation of the radius of a sphere will make it equivalent to any other sphere.

EXAMPLES

1) A square-based pyramid has a height of 10 cm. If the length of the side of the square is 6 cm, what is the surface area of the pyramid?

Answer:

GO ON

	The surface area will be the area of the square base plus the area of the four triangles.
$A = s^2$ $= 6^2 = 36$	Find the area of the square.
$c^2 = a^2 + b^2$ $\ell^2 = 100 + 9$ $\ell = \sqrt{109}$	To find the area of the triangles, first find the pyramid's slant height.
$A = \frac{1}{2} bh$ $A = \frac{1}{2}(6)(\sqrt{109})$ $A = 3\sqrt{109}$	Find the area of the triangle face using the slant height as the height of the triangle face.
$SA = 36 + 4(3\sqrt{109})$ **≈ 161.3 cm²**	Add the area of the square base and the four triangles to find the total surface area.

2) Given that two cones are similar and one cone's radius is three times longer than the other's radius, what is the volume of the smaller cone if the larger cone has a volume of 81π cubic inches and a height of 3 inches?

Answer:

$V_1 = 81\pi$ $h_1 = 3$	Identify the given variables.
$V_1 = \frac{1}{3}\pi r_1^2 h_1$ $81\pi = \frac{1}{3}\pi(r_1)(3)$ $r_1 = 9$	Find the radius of the larger cone with the given information.
$r_2 = \frac{1}{3} r_1$ $r_2 = \frac{1}{3}(9)$ $r_2 = 3$ $h_2 = \frac{1}{3} h_1$ $h_2 = \frac{1}{3}(3)$ $h_2 = 1$	Use the given scale factor to find the second cone's radius and height.

$V_2 = \frac{1}{3}\pi r_2^{2} h_2$ $V_2 = \frac{1}{3}\pi(3)^{2}(1)$ **$V_2 = 3\pi$**	Find the area of the smaller cone.

Triangle Congruence and Similarity

Congruence and similarity in triangles is governed by a set of theorems that make it easy to determine the relationship between two triangles. These theorems can be used by looking at the number and location of congruent sides and angles shared by the triangles.

Table 3.4. Triangle Congruence

	TRIANGLES ARE CONGRUENT IF...
SSS	all three corresponding sides are congruent.
SAS	two sides and the included angle are congruent.
AAS	two angles and one side are congruent.
ASA	two angles and the included side are congruent.

	TRIANGLES ARE SIMILAR IF...
AA	two angles (and thus the third) are congruent.
SAS	two sides are proportional and included angle is congruent.
SSS	the ratio between all three corresponding sides is constant.

A note of caution about the SSA case (also known as the ASS case): Two triangles that have congruent (or proportional) sides and one

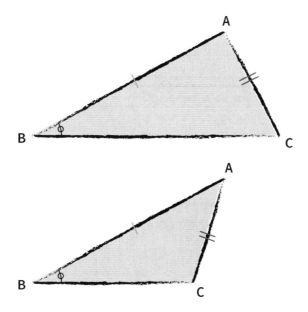

Figure 3.17. Two Possible Triangles Formed from Two Sides and One Non-Included Angle

congruent (but not included) angle are NOT necessarily congruent (or similar). This is because, given two side lengths and a nonincluded angle, it is often possible to draw an acute triangle and an obtuse triangle. Thus, there is NOT an SSA congruence theorem.

Right triangles, in general, have a couple of simpler similarity and congruence theorems. Since any pair of right triangles already has one angle that is the same (the right angle), any two pairs of corresponding sides that are either congruent or proportional will guarantee congruence or similarity between the triangles, respectively.

Table 3.5. Right Triangle Congruence

RIGHT TRIANGLES ARE CONGRUENT IF...	
HL	the hypotenuse and one leg are congruent.
LL	the two pairs of corresponding legs are congruent.

RIGHT TRIANGLES ARE SIMILAR IF...	
HL	the hypotenuse and one leg are proportional.
LL	two pairs of corresponding legs are similar.

EXAMPLES

1) Determine whether the following sets of triangles are congruent. If they are, state why.

A.   B.   C.   D.

Answer:

A. Not enough information is provided to determine if the triangles are congruent.

B. Congruent (ASA). The vertical angle shared by the triangles provides the second angle.

C. Congruent (SSS). The shared side is the third congruent side.

D. Not enough information is provided: SSA cannot be used to prove congruence.

2) If $\triangle ABC \sim \triangle DEF$, what is the length of $\overline{DE}$?

Answer:

Set up a proportion among the sides:

$$\frac{AB}{AC} = \frac{ED}{DF}$$

$$\frac{6}{7.5} = \frac{DE}{15}$$

$DE = 12$

Test Your Skills

1) Which of the angles in the figure below are congruent?

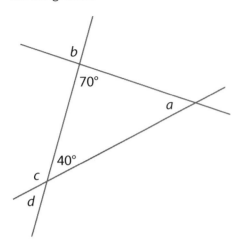

    A. *a* and *d*

    B. *b* and *d*

    C. *a* and *b*

    D. *c* and *b*

2) Which of the following could be the perimeter of a triangle with two sides that measure 13 and 5?

    A. 24.5

    B. 26.5

    C. 36

    D. 37

3) A cube is inscribed in a sphere such that each vertex on the cube touches the sphere. If the volume of the sphere is 972π cm³, what is the approximate volume of the cube in cubic centimeters?

    A. 9

    B. 10.4

    C. 1125

    D. 1729

4) If one leg of a right triangle has a length of 40, which of the following could be the lengths of the two remaining sides?

    A. 50 and 41

    B. 9 and 41

    C. 9 and 30

    D. 50 and 63

5) In the following graph of $f(x) = y$, for how many values of x does $|f(x)| = 1$?

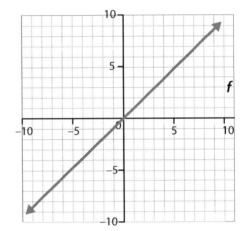

    A. 0

    B. 1

    C. 2

    D. ∞

6) Rectangular water tank A is 5 feet long, 10 feet wide, and 4 feet tall. Rectangular tank B is 5 feet long, 5 feet wide, and 4 feet tall. If the same amount of water is poured into both tanks and the height of the water in Tank A is 1 foot, how high will the water be in Tank B?

    A. 1 foot

    B. 2 feet

    C. 3 feet

    D. 4 feet

7) Two spheres are tangent to each other. One has a volume of 36π, and the other has a volume of 288π. What is the greatest distance between a point on one of the spheres and a point on the other sphere?

- **A.** 6
- **B.** 9
- **C.** 18
- **D.** 63

8) Which of the following sets of shapes are NOT all similar to each other?

- **A.** right triangles
- **B.** spheres
- **C.** 30–60–90 triangles
- **D.** squares

9) Cone A is similar to cone B with a scale factor of 3:4. If the volume of cone A is 54π, what is the volume of cone B?

Write in the answer: _____

10) W, X, Y, and Z lie on a circle with center A. If the diameter of the circle is 75, what is the sum of $\overline{AW}$, $\overline{AX}$, $\overline{AY}$, and $\overline{AZ}$?

Write in the answer: _____

Answer Key

1)   **C.** Find the measure of each angle.

$m\angle a = 180 - (70 + 40) = 70°$

$m\angle b = 70°$

$m\angle c = 180 - 40 = 140°$

$m\angle d = 40°$

$\angle a \cong \angle b$

2)   **B.** Use the triangle inequality theorem to find the possible values for the third side, then calculate the possible perimeters.

$13 - 5 < s < 13 + 5$

$8 < s < 18$

$13 + 5 + 8 < P < 13 + 5 + 18$

$26 < P < 36$

3)   **C.** Use the formula for the volume of a sphere to find its radius.

$V = \frac{4}{3}\pi r^3$

$972\pi = \frac{4}{3}\pi r^3$

$r = 9$

Use the super Pythagorean theorem to find the side of the cube.

$d^2 = a^2 + b^2 + c^2$

$18^2 = 3s^2$

$s \approx 10.4$

Use the length of the side to find the volume of the cube.

$V = s^3$

$V \approx (10.4)^3$

$V \approx 1,125$

4)   **B.** Use the Pythagorean theorem to determine which set of values forms a right triangle.

$40^2 + 41^2 = 50^2$

$3,281 \neq 2,500$

$9^2 + 40^2 = 41^2$

$1,681 = 1,681$

$9^2 + 30^2 = 40^2$

$981 \neq 1,600$

$40^2 + 50^2 = 63^2$

$4,100 \neq 3,969$

5)   **C.** The absolute value of $f(x)$ equals 1 twice: once in quadrant I and once in quadrant III.

6)   **B.** Calculate the volume of water in tank A.

$V = l \times w \times h$

$5 \times 10 \times 1 = 50 \text{ ft}^3$

Find the height this volume would reach in tank B.

$V = l \times w \times h$

$50 = 5 \times 5 \times h$

$h = \textbf{2 ft}$

7)   **C.** The greatest distance will be between two points at opposite ends of each sphere's diameters. Find the diameter of each sphere and add them.

$36\pi = \frac{4}{3}\pi r_1^3$

$r_1 = 3$

$d_1 = 2(3) = 6$

$288\pi = \frac{4}{3}\pi r_2^3$

$r_2 = 6$

$d_2 = 2(6) = 12$

$d_1 + d_1 = 6 + 12 = \textbf{18}$

8)   **A.** Corresponding angles in right triangles are not necessarily the same, so they do not have to be similar.

B. All spheres are similar.

C. Corresponding angles in 30–60–90 triangles are the same, so all 30–60–90 triangles are similar.

D. Corresponding angles in a square are all the same (90°), so all squares are similar.

9)   **B.** Set up a proportion. Cube the scale factor when calculating volume.

$\frac{54\pi}{x} = \frac{3^3}{4^3}$

$x = 128\pi$

10)   **C.** All the points lie on the circle, so each line segment is a radius. The sum of the 4 lines will be 4 times the radius.

$r = \frac{75}{2} = 37.5$

$4r = \mathbf{150}$

four

STATISTICS AND PROBABILITY

Describing Sets of Data

Measures of Central Tendency

Measures of central tendency help identify the center, or most typical, value within a data set. There are three such central tendencies that describe the "center" of the data in different ways. The MEAN is the arithmetic average and is found by dividing the sum of all measurements by the number of measurements. The mean of a population is written as μ and the mean of a sample is written as $\overline{x}$.

$$\text{population mean} = \mu = \frac{x_1 + x_2 + ...x_N}{N} = \frac{\Sigma x}{N}$$

$$\text{sample mean} = \overline{x} = \frac{x_1 + x_2 + ...x_n}{n} = \frac{\Sigma x}{n}$$

The data points are represented by x's with subscripts; the sum is denoted using the Greek letter sigma (Σ); N is the number of data points in the entire population; and n is the number of data points in a sample set.

The MEDIAN divides the measurements into two equal halves. The median is the measurement right in the middle of an odd set of measurements or the average of the two middle numbers in an even data set. When calculating the median, it is important to order the data values from least to greatest before attempting to locate the middle value. The MODE is simply the measurement that occurs most often. There can be many modes in a data set, or no mode. Since measures of central tendency describe a *center* of the data, all three of these measures will be between the lowest and highest data values (inclusive).

Unusually large or small values, called OUTLIERS, will affect the mean of a sample more than the mode. If there is a high outlier, the mean will be greater than the median; if there is a low outlier, the mean

When the same value is added to each term in a set, the mean increases by that value and the standard deviation is unchanged. When each term in a set is multiplied by the same value, both the mean and standard deviation will also be multiplied by that value.

will be lower than the median. When outliers are present, the median is a better measure of the data's center than the mean because the median will be closer to the terms in the data set.

EXAMPLES

1) What is the mean of the following data set? {1000, 0.1, 10, 1}

Answer:

Use the equation to find the mean of a sample:

$$\frac{1000 + 0.1 + 10 + 1}{4} = \textbf{252.78}$$

2) What is the median of the following data set? {1000, 10, 1, 0.1}

Answer:

Since there are an even number of data points in the set, the median will be the mean of the two middle numbers. Order the numbers from least to greatest: 0.1, 1, 10, and 1000. The two middle numbers are 1 and 10, and their mean is:

$$\frac{1 + 10}{2} = \textbf{5.5}$$

3) Josey has an average of 81 on four equally weighted tests she has taken in her statistics class. She wants to determine what grade she must receive on her fifth test so that her mean is 83, which will give her a B in the course, but she does not remember her other scores. What grade must she receive on her fifth test?

Answer:

Even though Josey does not know her test scores, she knows her average. Therefore it can be assumed that each test score was 81, since four scores of 81 would average to 81. To find the score, x, that she needs use the equation for the mean of a sample:

$$\frac{4(81) + x}{5} = 83$$

$$324 + x = 415$$

$$x = \textbf{91}$$

Measures of Variation

The values in a data set can be very close together (close to the mean), or very spread out. This is called the SPREAD or DISPERSION of the data. There are a few MEASURES OF VARIATION (or MEASURES OF DISPERSION) that quantify the spread within a data set. RANGE is the difference between the largest and smallest data points in a set:

R = largest data point – smallest data point

Notice range depends on only two data points (the two extremes). Sometimes these data points are outliers; regardless, for a large data set, relying on only two data points is not an exact tool.

The understanding of the data set can be improved by calculating QUARTILES. To calculate quartiles, first arrange the data in ascending order and find the set's median (also called quartile 2 or Q2). Then find the median of the lower half of the data, called quartile 1 (Q1), and the median of the upper half of the data, called quartile 3 (Q3). These three points divide the data into four equal groups of data (thus the word *quartile*). Each quartile contains 25% of the data.

INTERQUARTILE RANGE (IQR) provides a more reliable range that is not as affected by extremes. IQR is the difference between the third quartile data point and the first quartile data point and gives the spread of the middle 50% of the data:

$$IQR = Q_3 - Q_1$$

A measure of variation that depends on the mean is STANDARD DEVIATION, which uses every data point in a set and calculates the average distance of each data point from the mean of the data. Standard deviation can be computed for an entire population (written σ) or for a sample of a population (written s):

$$\sigma = \sqrt{\frac{\Sigma(x_i - \mu)^2}{N}} \qquad s = \sqrt{\frac{\Sigma(x_i - \bar{x})^2}{n - 1}}$$

Standard deviation and variance are also affected by extreme values. Though much simpler to calculate, interquartile range is the more accurate depiction of how the data is scattered when there are outlier values.

Thus, to calculate standard deviation, the difference between the mean and each data point is calculated. Each of these differences is squared (so that each is positive). The average of the squared values is computed by summing the squares and dividing by N or $(n - 1)$. Then the square root is taken, to "undo" the previous squaring.

The VARIANCE of a data set is simply the square of the standard variation:

$$V = \sigma^2 = \frac{1}{N} \sum_{i=1}^{N} (x_i - \mu)^2$$

Variance measures how narrowly or widely the data points are distributed. A variance of zero means every data point is the same; a large variance means there are a relatively small amount of data points near the set's mean.

EXAMPLES

1) What are the range and interquartile range of the following set? {3, 9, 49, 64, 81, 100, 121, 144, 169}

Answer:

R = largest point – smallest point = 169 – 3 = **166**	Use the equation for range.

3	
9	
$\rightarrow Q1 = \frac{49+9}{2} = 29$	
49	
64	Place the terms in numerical order and identify Q1, Q2, and Q3.
81 $\rightarrow$ Q2	
100	
121	
$\rightarrow Q3 = \frac{121+144}{2} = 132.5$	
144	
169	
IQR = Q3 − Q1	Find the IQR by subtracting Q1 from Q3.
= 132.5 − 29	
= **103.5**	

2) In a group of 7 people, 1 person has no children, 2 people have 1 child, 2 people have 2 children, 1 person has 5 children, and 1 person has 17 children. To the nearest hundredth of a child, what is the standard deviation in this group?

Answer:

$\{0, 1, 1, 2, 2, 5, 17\}$	Create a data set out of this scenario.
$\mu = \frac{x_1 + x_2 + \dots x_N}{N} = \frac{\Sigma x}{N}$	Calculate the population mean.
$\mu = \frac{0+1+1+2+2+5+17}{7} = 4$	
$(0-4)^2 = (-4)^2 = 16$	
$(1-4)^2 = (-3)^2 = 9$	
$(1-4)^2 = (-3)^2 = 9$	
$(2-4)^2 = (-2)^2 = 4$	Find the square of the difference of each term and the mean $(x_i - \mu)^2$.
$(2-4)^2 = (-2)^2 = 4$	
$(5-4)^2 = (1)^2 = 1$	
$(17-4)^2 = (13)^2 = 169$	
$\sigma = \sqrt{\frac{\Sigma(x_i - \mu)^2}{N}}$	Plug the sum (Σ) of these squares, 212, into the standard deviation formula.
$\sigma = \sqrt{\frac{212}{7}} = \sqrt{30.28} = \mathbf{5.50}$	

Box Plots

A box plot depicts the median and quartiles along a scaled number line. It is meant to summarize the data in a visual manner and emphasize central trends while decreasing the pull of outlier data. To construct a box plot:

1. Create a number line that begins at the lowest data point and terminates at the highest data point.

2. Find the quartiles of the data. Create a horizontal rectangle (the "box") whose left border is Q_1 and right border is Q_3.

3. Draw a vertical line within the box to mark the median.

4. Draw a horizontal line going from the left edge of the box to the smallest data value.

5. Draw a horizontal line going from the right edge of the box to the largest data value.

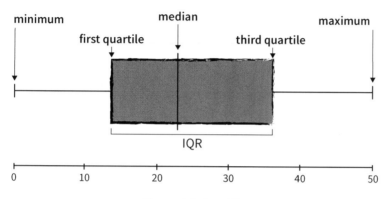

Figure 4.1. Box Plot

When reading a box plot, the following stands out:

♦ Reading from left to right: the horizontal line (whisker) shows the spread of the first quarter; the box's left compartment shows the spread of the second quarter; the box's right compartment shows the spread of the third quarter; and the right horizontal line shows the spread of the fourth quarter.

♦ The length of the box is the IQR, or the middle 50% of the data.

♦ Each of the four pieces (the whiskers and two pieces in the box) represent 25% of the data.

♦ If the median is skewed more toward the right, the second quartile has more data points in it; if the median is skewed more toward the left, the third quartile has more data points in it.

♦ The horizontal lines show by their length whether the data higher or lower than the middle 50% is prominent.

Box plots are also known as box-and-whisker plots, because if they are drawn correctly the two horizontal lines look like whiskers.

GO ON

A recent survey asked 8 people how many pairs of shoes they wear per week. Their answers are in the following data set: {1, 3, 5, 5, 7, 8, 12}. Construct a box plot from this data.

Answer:

Create a number line that begins at 1 and ends at 12. Q_1 is 3, the median (Q_2) is 5, and Q_3 is 8. A rectangle must be drawn whose length is 5 and that borders on Q_1 and Q_3. Mark the median of 5 within the rectangle. Draw a horizontal line going left to 1. Draw a horizontal line going right to 12.

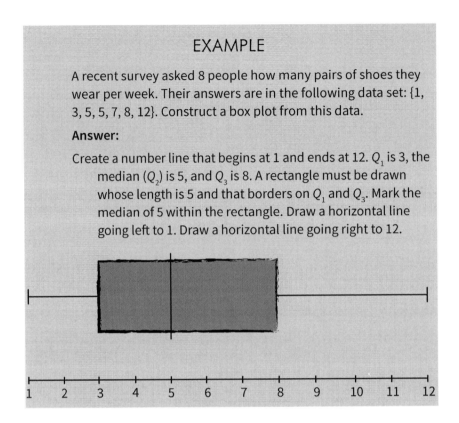

Graphs, Charts, and Tables

Pie Charts

A pie chart simply states the proportion of each category within the whole. To construct a pie chart, the categories of a data set must be determined. The frequency of each category must be found and that frequency converted to a percent of the total. To draw the pie chart, determine the angle of each slice by multiplying the percentage by 360°.

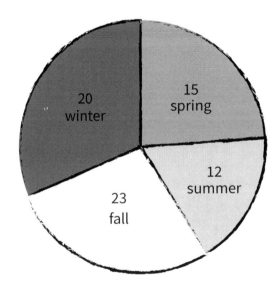

Figure 4.2. Pie Chart

EXAMPLE

A firm is screening applicants for a job by education-level attainment. There are 125 individuals in the pool: 5 have a doctorate, 20 have a master's degree, 40 have a bachelor's degree, 30 have an associate degree, and 30 have a high school degree. Construct a pie chart showing the highest level of education attained by the applicants.

Answer:

Create a frequency table to find the percentages and angle measurement for each category.

CATEGORY	FREQUENCY	PERCENT	ANGLE MEASURE
High School	30	24%	86.4
Associate	30	24%	86.4
Bachelor's	40	32%	115.2
Master's	20	16%	57.6
Doctorate	5	4%	14.4

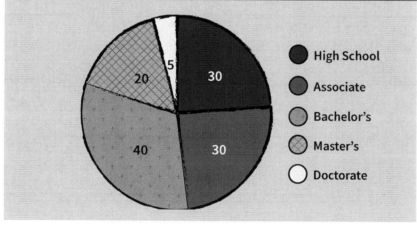

● High School
● Associate
● Bachelor's
● Master's
○ Doctorate

Scatter Plots

A scatter plot is displayed in the first quadrant of the *xy*-plane where all numbers are positive. Data points are plotted as ordered pairs, with one variable along the horizontal axis and the other along the vertical axis. Scatter plots can show if there is a correlation between two variables. There is a POSITIVE CORRELATION (expressed as a positive slope) if increasing one variable appears to result in an increase in the other variable. A NEGATIVE CORRELATION (expressed as a negative slope) occurs when an increase in one variable causes a decrease in the other. If the scatter plot shows no discernible pattern, then there is no correlation (a zero, mixed, or indiscernible slope).

Calculators or other software can be used to find the linear regression equation, which describes the general shape of the data. Graphing this equation produces the regression line, or line of best fit. The equation's **correlation coefficient** (r) can be used to determine how closely the equation fits the data. The value of r is between –1 and 1. The closer r is to 1 (if the line has a positive slope) or –1 (if the line has a negative slope), the better the regression line fits the data. The closer the r value is to 0, the weaker the correlation between the line and the data. Generally, if the absolute value of the correlation coefficient is 0.8 or higher, then it is considered to be a strong correlation, while an $|r|$ value of less than 0.5 is considered a weak correlation.

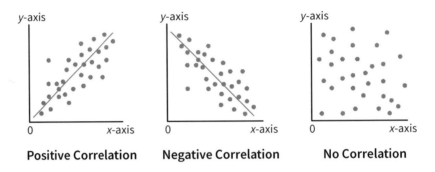

Figure 4.3. Scatter Plots and Correlation

To determine which curve is the "best fit" for a set of data, RESIDUALS are calculated. The calculator automatically calculates and saves these values to a list called RESID. These values are all the differences between the actual y-value of data points and the y-value calculated by the best-fit line or curve for that x-value. These values can be plotted on an xy-plane to produce a RESIDUAL PLOT. The residual plot helps determine if a line is the best model for the data. Residual points that are randomly dispersed above and below the horizontal indicate that a linear model is appropriate, while a u shape or upside-down u shape indicate a nonlinear model would be more appropriate.

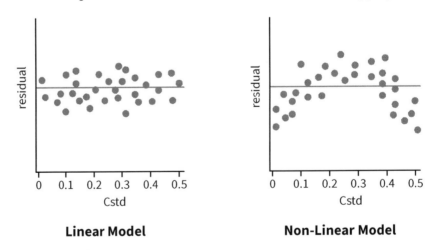

Figure 4.4. Residual Plots

Once a best-fit line is established, it can be used to estimate output values given an input value within the domain of the data. For a short extension outside that domain, reasonable predictions may be possible.

However, the further from the domain of the data the line is extended, the greater the reduction in the accuracy of the prediction.

It is important to note here that just because two variables have a strong positive or negative correlation, it cannot necessarily be inferred that those two quantities have a *causal* relationship—that is, that one variable changing *causes* the other quantity to change. There are often other factors that play into their relationship. For example, a positive correlation can be found between the number of ice cream sales and the number of shark attacks at a beach. It would be incorrect to say that selling more ice cream *causes* an increase in shark attacks. It is much more likely that on hot days more ice cream is sold, and many more people are swimming, so one of them is more likely to get attacked by a shark. Confusing correlation and causation is one of the most common statistical errors people make.

A graphing calculator can provide the regression line, r value, and residuals list.

EXAMPLE

Based on the scatter plot below, where the *x*-axis represents hours spent studying per week and the *y*-axis represents the average percent grade on exams during the school year, is there a correlation between the amount of studying for a test and test results?

Answer:

There is a somewhat weak positive correlation. As the number of hours spent studying increases, the average percent grade also generally increases.

Line Graphs

Line graphs are used to display a relationship between two variables, such as change over time. Like scatter plots, line graphs exist in quadrant I of the *xy*-plane. Line graphs are constructed by graphing each point and connecting each point to the next consecutive point by a line. To create a line graph, it may be necessary to consolidate data into single bivariate data points. Thus, a line graph is a function, with each *x*-value having exactly one *y*-value, whereas a scatter plot may have multiple *y*-values for one *x*-value.

Figure 4.5. Line Graph

EXAMPLE

Create a line graph based on the following survey values, where the first column represents an individual's age and the other represents that individual's reported happiness level on a 20-point scale (0 being the least happy that person has been and 20 being the happiest). Then interpret the resulting graph to determine whether the following statement is true or false: *On average, middle-aged people are less happy than young or older people are.*

Age	Happiness
12	16
13	15
20	18
15	12
40	5
17	17
18	18
19	15
42	7
70	17
45	10
60	12
63	15
22	14
27	15

Age	Happiness
33	10
44	8
55	10
80	10
15	13
40	8
17	15
18	17
19	20
22	16
27	15
36	9
33	10
44	6

Answer:

To construct a line graph, the data must be ordered into consolidated categories by averaging the data of people who have the same age so that the data is one-to-one. For example, there are 2 twenty-two-year-olds who are reporting. Their average happiness level is 15. When all the data has been consolidated and ordered from least to greatest, the table and graph below can be presented.

Age	Happiness
12	16
13	15
15	12.5
17	16
18	17.5
19	17.5
20	18
22	15
27	15
33	10
36	10.5
40	6.5
42	7
44	7
45	10
55	10

AGE	HAPPINESS
60	12
63	15
70	17
80	10

Average Happiness Rating Versus Age

The statement that, on average, middle-aged people are less happy than young or older people appears to be true. According to the graph, people in their thirties, forties, and fifties are less happy than people in their teens, twenties, sixties, and seventies.

Bar Graphs

Bar graphs compare differences between categories or changes over a time. The data is grouped into categories or ranges and represented by rectangles. A bar graph's rectangles can be vertical or horizontal, depending on whether the dependent variable is placed on the *x*- or *y*-axis. Instead of the *xy*-plane, however, one axis is made up of categories (or ranges) instead of a numeric scale. Bar graphs are useful

Figure 4.6. Bar Graph

because the differences between categories are easy to see: the height or length of each bar shows the value for each category.

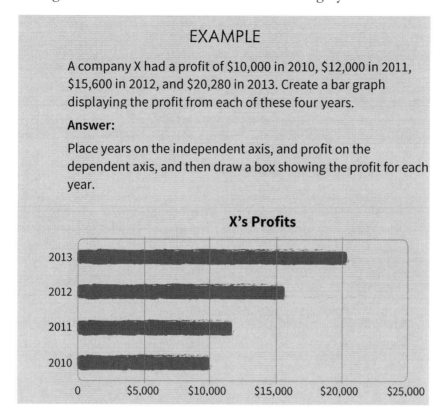

EXAMPLE

A company X had a profit of $10,000 in 2010, $12,000 in 2011, $15,600 in 2012, and $20,280 in 2013. Create a bar graph displaying the profit from each of these four years.

Answer:

Place years on the independent axis, and profit on the dependent axis, and then draw a box showing the profit for each year.

Stem-and-Leaf Plots

Stem-and-leaf plots are ways of organizing large amounts of data by grouping it into classes. All data points are broken into two parts: a stem and a leaf. For instance, the number 512 might be broken into a stem of 5 and a leaf of 12. All data in the 500 range would appear in the same row (this group of data is a class). Usually a simple key is provided to explain how the data is being represented. For instance, $5|12 = 512$ would show that the stems are representing hundreds. The advantage of this display is that it shows general density and shape of the data in a compact display, yet all original data points are preserved and available. It is also easy to find medians and quartiles from this display.

Stem	Leaf
0	5
1	6, 7
2	8, 3, 6
3	4, 5, 9, 5, 5, 8, 5
4	7, 7, 7, 8
5	5, 4
6	0

Figure 4.7. Stem and Leaf Plot

EXAMPLE

The table gives the weights of wrestlers (in pounds) for a certain competition. What is the mean, median, and IQR of the data?

2	05, 22, 53, 40
3	07, 22, 29, 45, 89, 96, 98
4	10, 25, 34
6	21

Key: 2|05 = 205 pounds

Answer:

$\mu = \dfrac{\Sigma x}{N}$ $= \dfrac{5281}{15}$ **= 353.1 lbs.**	Find the mean using the equation for the population mean.
Q1 = 240 Q2 = 345 Q3 = 410 IQR = 410 – 240 = 170 **The median is 345 lbs.** **The IQR is 170 lbs.**	Find the median and IQR by counting the leaves and identifying Q1, Q2, and Q3.

Frequency Tables and Histograms

The frequency of a particular data point is the number of times that data point occurs. Constructing a frequency table requires that the data or data classes be arranged in ascending order in one column and the frequency in another column.

A histogram is a graphical representation of a frequency table used to compare frequencies. A histogram is constructed in quadrant I of the *xy*-plane, with data in each equal-width class presented as a bar and the height of each bar representing the frequency of that class. Unlike bar graphs, histograms cannot have gaps between bars. A histogram is used to determine the distribution of data among the classes.

Histograms can be symmetrical, skewed left or right, or multimodal (data spread around). Note that SKEWED LEFT means the peak of the data is on the *right*, with a tail to the left, while SKEWED RIGHT means the peak is on the *left*, with a tail to the right. This seems counterintuitive to many; the "left" or "right" always refers to the tail of the data. This is because a long tail to the right, for example, means there are high outlier values that are skewing the data to the right.

Bar Chart

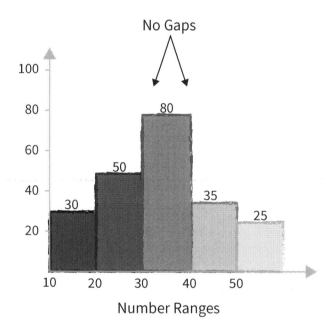

Histogram

Figure 4.8. Bar Chart vs. Histogram

A TWO-WAY FREQUENCY TABLE compares CATEGORICAL DATA (data in more than one category) of two related variables (bivariate data). Two-way frequency tables are also called CONTINGENCY TABLES and are often used to analyze survey results. One category is displayed along the top of the table and the other category down along the side. Rows and columns are added and the sums appear at the end of the row or column. The sum of all the row data must equal the sum of all the column data.

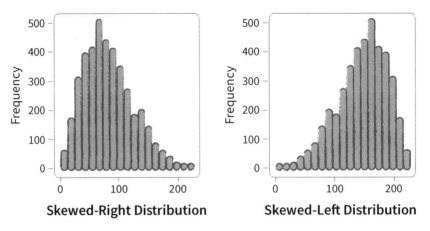

Figure 4.9. Histrograms

From a two-way frequency table, the JOINT RELATIVE FREQUENCY of a particular category can be calculated by taking the number in the row and column of the categories in question and dividing by the total number surveyed. This gives the percent of the total in that particular category. Sometimes the CONDITIONAL RELATIVE FREQUENCY is of interest. In this case, calculate the relative frequency confined to a single row or column.

Students by Grade and Gender

	9TH GRADE	10TH GRADE	11TH GRADE	12TH GRADE	TOTAL
Male	57	63	75	61	256
Female	54	42	71	60	227
Total	111	105	146	121	483

Figure 4.10. Two-Way Frequency Table

EXAMPLES

1) A café owner tracked the number of customers he had over a twelve-hour period in the following frequency table. Display the data in a histogram and determine what kind of distribution there is in the data.

TIME	NUMBER OF CUSTOMERS
6 a.m. – 8 a.m.	5
8 a.m. – 9 a.m.	6
9 a.m. – 10 a.m.	5
10 a.m. – 12 p.m.	23

Time	Number of Customers
12 p.m. – 2 p.m.	24
2 p.m. – 4 p.m.	9
4 p.m. – 6 p.m.	4

Answer:

Since time is the independent variable, it is on the *x*-axis and the number of customers is on the *y*-axis. For the histogram to correctly display data continuously, categories on the *x*-axis must be equal 2-hour segments. The 8 a.m. – 9 a.m. and 9 a.m. – 10 a.m. categories must be combined for a total of 11 customers in that time period. Although not perfectly symmetrical, the amount of customers peaks in the middle and is therefore considered symmetrical.

2) Cineflix movie theater polled its moviegoers on a weeknight to determine their favorite type of movie. The results are in the two-way frequency table below.

Moviegoers	Comedy	Action	Horror	Totals
Male	15	24	21	60
Female	8	18	17	43
Totals	23	42	38	103

Determine whether each of the following statements is true or false.

A. Men choose the horror genre more frequently than women do.

B. Action films are the most popular type of movie offered.

C. About 1 in 5 moviegoers prefers comedy films.

Answer:

A. **True**. More people (43) chose action movies than comedy (23) or horror (38).

B. **True.** Use the equation for percentages to find the percentage of female moviegoers who prefer action films:

part = number of women who prefer action = 18

whole = number of women surveyed = 43

$percent = \dfrac{part}{whole}$

$= \dfrac{18}{43} = 0.42 = 42\%$

C. **False.** The percentage of men who choose horror is less than the percentage of women who do.

part = number of men who prefer horror =21

whole = number of men surveyed = 60

$percent = \dfrac{part}{whole}$

$= \dfrac{21}{60} = 0.35 = 35\%$

part = number of women who prefer horror =17

whole = number of women surveyed = 43

$percent = \dfrac{part}{whole}$

$= \dfrac{17}{43} = 0.40 = 40\%$

Probability

robability describes how likely something is to happen. In probability, an **EVENT** is the single result of a trial, and an **OUTCOME** is a possible event that results from a trial. The collection of all possible outcomes for a particular trial is called the **SAMPLE SPACE**. For example, when rolling a die, the sample space is the numbers 1 – 6. Rolling a single number, such as 4, would be a single event.

Counting Principles

Counting principles are methods used to find the number of possible outcomes for a given situation. The **FUNDAMENTAL COUNTING PRINCIPLE** states that, for a series of independent events, the number of outcomes can be found by multiplying the number of possible outcomes for each event. For example, if a die is rolled (6 possible outcomes) and a coin is tossed (2 possible outcomes), there are 6 × 2 = 12 total possible outcomes.

Combinations and permutations describe how many ways a number of objects taken from a group can be arranged. The number of objects in the group is written *n*, and the number of objects to be arranged is represented by *r* (or *k*). In a **COMBINATION**, the order of the selections does not matter because every available slot to be filled is the same. Examples of combinations include:

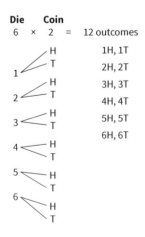

Figure 4.10. Fundamental Counting Principle

- picking 3 people from a group of 12 to form a committee (220 possible committees)
- picking 3 pizza toppings from 10 options (120 possible pizzas)

In a **PERMUTATION**, the order of the selection matters, meaning each available slot is different. Examples of permutations include:

- handing out gold, silver, and bronze medals in a race with 100 participants (970,200 possible combinations)
- selecting a president, vice-president, secretary, and treasurer from among a committee of 12 people (11,880 possible combinations)

The formulas for the both calculations are similar. The only difference—the $r!$ in the denominator of a combination—accounts for redundant outcomes. Note that both permutations and combinations can be written in several different shortened notations.

$$\text{Permutation: } P(n, r) = {}_nP_r = \frac{n!}{(n - r)!}$$

$$\text{Combination: } C(n, r) = {}_nC_r = \left(\frac{n}{r}\right) = \frac{n!}{(n - r)!r!}$$

EXAMPLES

1) A personal assistant is struggling to pick a shirt, tie, and cufflink set that go together. If his client has 70 shirts, 2 ties, and 5 cufflinks, how many possible combinations does he have to consider?

   Answer:

   Multiply the number of outcomes for each individual event:

   $(70)(2)(5) =$ **700 outfits**

2) If there are 20 applicants for 3 open positions, in how many different ways can a team of 3 be hired?

   Answer:

   The order of the items doesn't matter, so use the formula for combinations:

   $$C(n, r) = \frac{n!}{(n - r)!r!}$$

   $$C(20, 3) = \frac{20!}{(20 - 3)!3!}$$

   $$= \frac{20!}{(17!\,3!)}$$

   $$= \frac{(20)(19)(18)}{3!} = \textbf{1140 possible teams}$$

3) Calculate the number of unique permutations that can be made with five of the letters in the word *pickle*.

   Answer:

To find the number of unique permutations of 5 letters in pickle, use the permutation formula:

$$P(n,r) = \frac{n!}{(n-r)!}$$

$$P(6,5) = \frac{6!}{(6-5)!}$$

$$= \frac{720}{1} = \mathbf{720}$$

4) Find the number of permutations that can be made out of all the letters in the word *cheese*.

Answer:

The letter *e* repeats 3 times in the word *cheese*, meaning some permutations of the 6 letters will be indistinguishable from others. The number of permutations must be divided by the number of ways the three *e*'s can be arranged to account for these redundant outcomes:

$$total\ number\ of\ permutations = \frac{number\ of\ ways\ of\ arranging\ 6\ letters}{number\ of\ ways\ of\ arranging\ 3\ letters}$$

$$= \frac{6!}{3!} = 6 \times 5 \times 4 = \mathbf{120}$$

Probability of a Single Event

The probability of a single event occurring is the number of outcomes in which that event occurs (called **FAVORABLE EVENTS**) divided by the number of items in the sample space (total possible outcomes):

$$P\ (an\ event) = \frac{number\ of\ favorable\ outcomes}{total\ number\ of\ possible\ outcomes}$$

The probability of any event occurring will always be a fraction or decimal between 0 and 1. It may also be expressed as a percent. An event with 0 probability will never occur and an event with a probability of 1 is certain to occur. The probability of an event not occurring is referred to as that event's **COMPLEMENT**. The sum of an event's probability and the probability of that event's complement will always be 1.

EXAMPLES

1) What is the probability that an even number results when a six-sided die is rolled? What is the probability the die lands on 5?

Answer:

$$P(rolling\ even) = \frac{number\ of\ favorable\ outcomes}{total\ number\ of\ possible\ outcomes} = \frac{3}{6} = \frac{1}{2}$$

$$P(rolling\ 5) = \frac{number\ of\ favorable\ outcomes}{total\ number\ of\ possible\ outcomes} = \mathbf{\frac{1}{6}}$$

2) Only 20 tickets were issued in a raffle. If someone were to buy 6 tickets, what is the probability that person would not win the raffle?

Answer:

$$P(not\ winning) = \frac{number\ of\ favorable\ outcomes}{total\ number\ of\ possible\ outcomes} = \frac{14}{20} = \frac{7}{10}$$

or

$$P(\text{not winning}) = 1 - P(\text{winning}) = 1 - \frac{6}{20} = \frac{14}{20} = \frac{7}{10}$$

3) A bag contains 26 tiles representing the 26 letters of the English alphabet. If 3 tiles are drawn from the bag without replacement, what is the probability that all 3 will be consonants?

Answer:

$$P = \frac{number\ of\ favorable\ outcomes}{total\ number\ of\ possible\ outcomes}$$

$$= \frac{number\ of\ 3\text{-}consonant\ combinations}{number\ of\ 3\text{-}tile\ combinations}$$

$$= \frac{_{21}C_3}{_{26}C_3}$$

$$= \frac{54,264}{65,780}$$

$$= 0.82 = \mathbf{82\%}$$

Probability of Multiple Events

If events are INDEPENDENT, the probability of one occurring does not affect the probability of the other event occurring. Rolling a die and getting one number does not change the probability of getting any particular number on the next roll. The number of faces has not changed, so these are independent events.

If events are DEPENDENT, the probability of one occurring changes the probability of the other event occurring. Drawing a card from a deck without replacing it will affect the probability of the next card drawn because the number of available cards has changed.

To find the probability that two or more independent events will occur (A and B), simply multiply the probabilities of each individual event together. To find the probability that one, the other, or both will occur (A or B), it's necessary to add their probabilities and then subtract their overlap (which prevents the same values from being counted twice).

CONDITIONAL PROBABILITY is the probability of an event occurring given that another event has occurred. The notation $P(B|A)$ represents the probability that event B occurs, given that event A has already occurred (it is read "probability of B, given A").

When drawing objects, the phrase *with replacement* describes independent events, and *without replacement* describes dependent events.

Table 4.1. Probability Formulas

INDEPENDENT EVENTS		DEPENDENT EVENTS
Intersection *and*	Union *or*	Conditional
$P(A \cap B) = P(A) \times P(B)$	$P(A \cup B) = P(A) + P(B) - P(A \cap B)$	$P(B|A) = P(A \cap B)/P(A)$

Two events that are MUTUALLY EXCLUSIVE CANNOT happen at the same time. This is similar to disjoint sets in set theory. The probability that two mutually exclusive events will occur is zero. MUTUALLY INCLUSIVE events share common outcomes.

EXAMPLES

1) A card is drawn from a standard 52 card deck. What is the probability that it is either a queen or a heart?

Answer:

This is a union (*or*) problem.

$P(A)$ = the probability of drawing a queen = $\frac{1}{13}$

$P(B)$ = the probability of drawing a heart = $\frac{1}{4}$

$P(A \cap B)$ = the probability of drawing a heart and a queen = $\frac{1}{52}$

$P(A \cup B) = P(A) + P(B) - P(A \cap B)$

$= \frac{1}{13} + \frac{1}{4} - \frac{1}{52}$

$= \mathbf{0.31}$

2) A group of ten individuals is drawing straws from a group of 28 long straws and 2 short straws. If the straws are not replaced, what is the probability, as a percentage, that neither of the first two individuals will draw a short straw?

Answer:

This scenario includes two events, A and B.

The probability of the first person drawing a long straw is an independent event:

$P(A) = \frac{28}{30}$

The probability the second person draws a long straw changes because one long straw has already been drawn. In other words, it is the probability of event B given that event A has already happened:

$P(B|A) = \frac{27}{29}$

The conditional probability formula can be used to determine the probability of both people drawing long straws:

$P(A \cap B) = P(A)P(B|A)$

$= \left(\frac{28}{30}\right)\left(\frac{27}{29}\right)$

$= 0.87$

There is an **87% chance** that neither of the first two individuals will draw short straws.

Test Your Skills

1) The pie graph below shows how a state's government plans to spend its annual budget of $3 billion. How much more money does the state plan to spend on infrastructure than education?

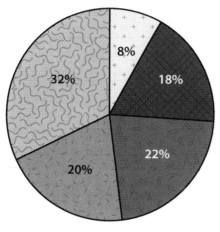

⊕ Employees   ⬤ Education

⬤ Healthcare   ◍ Pension

◍ Infrastructure

- **A.** $60,000,000
- **B.** $120,000,000
- **C.** $300,000,000
- **D.** $600,000,000

2) What is the relationship between the mean and the median in a data set that is skewed right?

- **A.** The mean is greater than the median.
- **B.** The mean is less than the median.
- **C.** The mean and median are equal.
- **D.** The mean may be greater than, less than, or equal to the median.

3) During a basketball tournament, Peter places a $40 bet on each game and has a 20% chance of winning in each game. If he starts with $160, what is the probability that he has money left after betting on 4 games?

- **A.** $\frac{1}{625}$
- **B.** $\frac{256}{625}$
- **C.** $\frac{369}{625}$
- **D.** $\frac{1}{8}$

4) A company interviewed 21 applicants for a recent opening. Of these applicants, 7 wore blue and 6 wore white, while 5 applicants wore both blue and white. What is the number of applicants who wore neither blue nor white?

- **A.** 1
- **B.** 6
- **C.** 12
- **D.** 13

5) In a class of 20 students, how many conversations must be had so that every student talks to every other student in the class?

- **A.** 190
- **B.** 380
- **C.** 760
- **D.** 6840

6) How many unique ways can the letters in the word *FOGGIER* be arranged?

- **A.** 42
- **B.** 1050
- **C.** 2520
- **D.** 5040

7) Which data set has a median larger than the mean and a standard deviation less than 2?

    A. {5, 5, 5, 5, 5, 5}

    B. {0, 0, 2, 8, 8, 8}

    C. {1, 1, 5, 5, 10, 20}

    D. {1, 2, 5, 5, 5, 6}

8) A bag contains 6 blue, 8 silver, and 4 green marbles. Two marbles are drawn from the bag. What is the probability that the second marble drawn will be green if replacement is not allowed?

    A. $\frac{2}{9}$

    B. $\frac{4}{17}$

    C. $\frac{11}{17}$

    D. $\frac{7}{9}$

9) A restaurant offers burritos on a corn or a flour tortilla, 5 types of meat, 6 types of cheese, and 3 different toppings. When ordering, customers can choose 1 type of tortilla, 1 meat, and 1 cheese. They can then add any of the 3 toppings. How many different burrito combinations are possible?

Write in the answer: _____

10) The mean of 13 numbers is 30. The mean of 8 of these numbers is 42. What is the mean of the other 5 numbers?

Write in the answer: _____

GO ON

Answer Key

1) **A.** Find the amount the state will spend on infrastructure and education, and then find the difference.

infrastructure = 0.2(3,000,000,000) = 600,000,000

education = 0.18(3,000,000,000) = 540,000,000

600,000,000 − 540,000,000 = **$60,000,000**

2) **A.** If the data is skewed right, the set includes extremes values that are to the right, or high. The median is unaffected by these high values, but the mean includes these high values and would therefore be greater.

3) **C.** Deterine the probability that Peter will lose in all four games and subtract from 1 to find the probability that he will have won at least one bet (and thus will have money left).

probability of losing = 80% = $\frac{4}{5}$

$\frac{4}{5} \times \frac{4}{5} \times \frac{4}{5} \times \frac{4}{5} = \frac{256}{625}$

probability of winning at least once = $1 - \frac{256}{625} = \frac{369}{625}$

4) **D.** Set up an equation to find the number of people wearing neither white nor blue. Subtract the number of people wearing both colors so they are not counted twice.

21 = 7 + 6 + *neither* − 5

neither = **13**

5) **A.** Use the combination formula to find the number of ways to choose 2 people out of a group of 20.

$C(20, 2) = \frac{20!}{2! \, 18!} = \textbf{190}$

6) **C.** Use the fundamental counting principle to find the number of ways the letters can be arranged. Because the two G's are indistinguishable, divide by the number of ways those 2 letters can be arranged.

$\frac{7!}{2!} = (7)(6)(5)(4)(3) = \textbf{2520}$

7) **D.** This problem can be solved by calculating the needed values, but it's faster to examine the general shape of each data set.

A. is incorrect: All the values are the same, so the mean and median will have the same value.

B. is incorrect: The majority of the data points are not close to the mean, so the standard deviation will be high.

C. is incorrect: The high outlier will make the mean larger than the median.

D. is correct: The mean is slightly lower than the median, and the spread is small.

8) **A.** Find the probability that the second marble will be green if the first marble is blue, silver, or green, and then add these probabilities together.

P(first blue and second green) = P(blue) × P(green|first blue) = $\frac{6}{18} \times \frac{4}{17} = \frac{4}{51}$

P(first silver and second green) = P(silver) × P(green|first silver) = $\frac{8}{18} \times \frac{4}{17} = \frac{16}{153}$

P(first green and second green) = P(green) × P(green|first green) = $\frac{4}{18} \times \frac{3}{17} = \frac{2}{51}$

P(second green) = $\frac{4}{51} + \frac{16}{153} + \frac{2}{51} = \frac{2}{9}$

9) Use the fundamental counting principle. Each topping has two possible choices (yes or no).

2(5)(6)(2)(2)(2) = **480**

10) Find the sum of the 13 numbers whose mean is 30: 13 × 30 = 390

Find the sum of the 8 numbers whose mean is 42: 8 × 42 = 336

Find the sum and mean of the remaining 5 numbers. 390 − 336 = 54

$\frac{54}{5} = \textbf{10.8}$

five

PRACTICE TEST

Multiple Choice

Directions: Read the problem carefully, and choose the best answer.

1. Simplify: $(5 + 2i)(3 + 4i)$

    A) 7

    B) 23

    C) $7 + 26i$

    D) $23 + 26i$

2. The average speed of cars on a highway (s) is inversely proportional to the number of cars on the road (n). If a car drives at 65 mph when there are 250 cars on the road, how fast will a car drive when there are 325 cars on the road?

    A) 50 mph

    B) 55 mph

    C) 60 mph

    D) 85 mph

3. What is the total number of 6-digit numbers in which each individual digit is less than 3 or greater than 6?

    A) 38,880

    B) 46,656

    C) 80,452

    D) 101,370

4. Line a and line b are perpendicular and intersect at the point $(-100, 100)$. If $(-95, 115)$ is a point on line b, which of the following could be a point on line a?

    A) $(104, 168)$

    B) $(-95, 115)$

    C) $(-112, 104)$

    D) $(-112, -104)$

5. Simplify: $\dfrac{7.2 \times 10^6}{1.6 \times 10^{-3}}$

    A) 4.5×10^{-9}

    B) 4.5×10^{-3}

    C) 4.5×10^{3}

    D) 4.5×10^{9}

6. Which of the following is the y-intercept of the given equation?

$7y - 42x + 7 = 0$

    A) $(0, \frac{1}{6})$

    B) $(6, 0)$

    C) $(0, -1)$

    D) $(-1, 0)$

7. The coordinates of point A are $(7, 12)$ and the coordinates of point C are $(-3, 10)$. If C is the midpoint of $\overline{AB}$, what are the coordinates of point B?

A) $(2, 11)$

B) $(-13, 8)$

C) $(17, 14)$

D) $(-13, 11)$

8. A data set contains information on the hours worked in a government department. Which of the following statistics would have a unit that is NOT hours?

A) variance

B) standard deviation

C) range

D) interquartile range

9. Which of the following is equivalent to $z^3(z + 2)^2 - 4z^3 + 2$?

A) 2

B) $z^5 + 4z^4 + 4z^3 + 2$

C) $z^6 + 4z^3 + 2$

D) $z^5 + 4z^4 + 2$

10. Which of the following represents a linear equation?

A) $\sqrt[3]{y} = x$

B) $\sqrt[3]{x} = y$

C) $\sqrt[3]{y} = x^2$

D) $y = \sqrt[3]{x^3}$

11. If the length of a rectangle is increased by 40% and its width is decreased by 40%, what is the effect on the rectangle's area?

A) The area is the same.

B) It increases by 16%.

C) It increases by 20%.

D) It decreases by 16%.

12. Simplify: $-(3^2) + (5 - 7)^2 - 3(4 - 8)$

A) -17

B) -1

C) 7

D) 25

13. What is the value of z in the following system?

$z - 2x = 14$

$2z - 6x = 18$

A) -7

B) 3

C) 5

D) 24

14. What is the approximate value of a in the triangle below if b is $\frac{7}{8}$ the value of a?

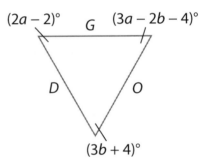

A) ≈ 22

B) ≈ 30

C) ≈ 31

D) ≈ 42

15. 50 shares of a financial stock and 10 shares of an auto stock are valued at $1,300. If 10 shares of the financial stock and 10 shares of the auto stock are valued at $500, what is the value of 50 shares of the auto stock?

A) $30

B) $20

C) $1,300

D) $1,500

16. 600 people between the ages of 15 and 45 were polled regarding their use of social media. 200 people from each age group were part of the study. The results are listed in the relative frequency table below.

Hours Per Day Spent on Social Media

AGE (YEARS)	LESSTHAN2HOURS	2 TO 4 HOURS	MORETHAN4HOURS	TOTAL
15 – 25	0.15	0.40	0.45	1.0
25 – 35	0.52	0.28	0.20	1.0
35 – 45	0.85	0.10	0.05	1.0
Total	0.51	0.26	0.23	1.0

Which of the statements are true?

I. Of people 25 to 35 years old, 20% spend more than 4 hours per day on social media.

II. Of the population of 15 to 45-year-olds, 26% spend 2 – 4 hours a day on social media.

III. Of people between the ages of 15 and 35, 67% spend 0 – 2 hours per day on social media.

IV. 5 people who reported using social media more than 4 hours per week were 35 to 45 years old.

A) I and II

B) I, II, and IV

C) I, II, and III

D) II, III, and IV

17. If a person reads 40 pages in 45 minutes, approximately how many minutes will it take her to read 265 pages?

A) 202

B) 236

C) 265

D) 298

18. $\overline{MN}$ is the diameter of circle O. If the coordinates of M are $(4, 5)$ and the coordiantes of N are $(-12, -11)$, what is the equation for circle O?

A) $(x + 4)^2 + (y + 3)^2 = 100$

B) $(x - 4)^2 + (y - 3)^2 = 10$

C) $(x + 4)^2 + (y - 3)^2 = 10$

D) $(x - 4)^2 + (y + 3)^2 = 100$

19. Find the approximate value of x in the triangle below.

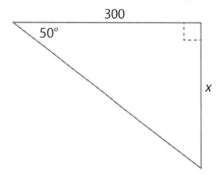

A) 229

B) 300

C) 357

D) 400

20. A pair of 6-sided dice is rolled 10 times. What is the probability that in exactly 3 of those rolls, the sum of the dice will be 5?

A) 0.14%

B) 7.2%

C) 11.1%

D) 60%

21. A wedge from a cylindrical piece of cheese was cut as shown. If the entire wheel of cheese weighed 73 pounds before the wedge was removed, what is the approximate remaining weight of the cheese?

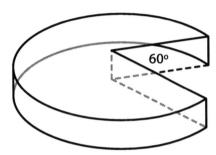

A) 12.17 pounds

B) 37.00 pounds

C) 60.83 pounds

D) 66.92 pounds

22. Which of the following is the solution set to the given inequality?

$2x + 4 \geq 5(x - 4) - 3(x - 4)$

A) $(-\infty, \infty)$

B) $(-\infty, 6.5]$

C) $[6.5, -\infty)$

D) $(-\infty, 6.5) \cup (6.5, \infty)$

23. What is the axis of symmetry for the given parabola?

$y = -2(x + 3)^2 + 5$

A) $y = 3$

B) $x = -3$

C) $y = -3$

D) $x = 3$

24. The population of a town was 7,250 in 2014 and 7,375 in 2015. What was the percent increase from 2014 to 2015 to the nearest tenth of a percent?

A) 1.5%

B) 1.6%

C) 1.7%

D) 1.8%

25. What are the real zero(s) of the following polynomial?

$2n^2 + 2n - 12 = 0$

A) $\{2\}$

B) $\{-3, 2\}$

C) $\{2, 4\}$

D) There are no real zeros of n.

26. Which of the following is the vertical asymptote of the function

$f(x) = \frac{x + 4}{-2x - 6}$?

A) $y = \frac{1}{2}$

B) $y = -2$

C) $x = 3$

D) $x = -3$

27. The line of best fit is calculated for a data set that tracks the number of miles that passenger cars traveled annually in the US from 1960 to 2010. In the model, $x = 0$ represents the year 1960, and y is the number of miles traveled in billions. If the line of best fit is $y = 0.0293x + 0.563$, approximately how many additional miles were traveled for every 5 years that passed?

A) 0.0293 billion

B) 0.1465 billion

C) 0.563 billion

D) 0.710 billion

28. In the *xy*-coordinate plane, how many points have a distance of four from the origin?

A) 0

B) 2

C) 4

D) ∞

29. Which inequality is represented by the following graph?

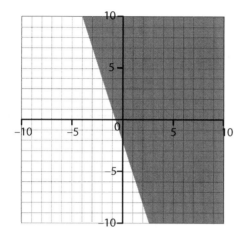

A) $y \geq -3x - 2$

B) $y \geq 3x - 2$

C) $y > -3x - 2$

D) $y \leq -3x - 2$

30. Simplify: $\left(\dfrac{4x^{-3}y^4z^2}{8x^{-5}y^3z^{-2}}\right)^2$

A) $\dfrac{x^4yz^3}{2}$

B) $\dfrac{x^4y^2z^6}{2}$

C) $\dfrac{x^4y^2z^6}{4}$

D) $\dfrac{x^4yz^3}{4}$

31. Find $(f - g)(x)$ if $f(x) = x^2 + 16x$ and $g(x) = 5x^2 + 4x + 25$.

A) $-4x^2 + 12x - 25$

B) $-4x^2 - 12x - 25$

C) $-4x^2 - 20x + 25$

D) $4x^2 - 20x - 25$

32. Based on the box plot below, which statement is false?

Heights of Buildings on a City Block
(meters)

A) There is a building on the block that is exactly 350 meters.

B) The difference between the tallest and shortest buliding is 400 meters.

C) 75% of the buildings are 450 meters or less tall.

D) The middle 50% of buildings is between 250 and 450 meters.

33. If the perimeter of an equilateral triangle is 30 inches, what is the altitude of the triangle?

A) 5

B) $5\sqrt{3}$

C) 10

D) $15\sqrt{3}$

34. Simplify: $\dfrac{3+\sqrt{3}}{4-\sqrt{3}}$

A) $\dfrac{13}{15}$

B) $\dfrac{15+7\sqrt{3}}{13}$

C) $\dfrac{15}{19}$

D) $\dfrac{15+7\sqrt{3}}{19}$

35. What is the domain of the inequality $\left|\dfrac{x}{8}\right| \geq 1$?

A) $(-\infty, \infty)$

B) $[8, \infty)$

C) $(-\infty, -8]$

D) $(-\infty, -8] \cup [8, \infty)$

36. From 2009 to 2015, what is the average number of months that Chicago had 3 or less inches of rain?

Number of Months with 3 or Fewer Than 3 Inches of Rain

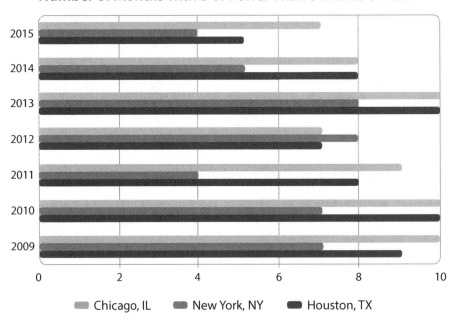

A) 6

B) 7

C) 8

D) 9

37. Which expression is equivalent to $\log_6\left(\frac{36}{x}\right)$?

A) $2 - x$

B) $6 - \log x$

C) $2 - \log_6 x$

D) $\log_6 x - 2$

38. If the surface area of a cylinder with radius of 4 feet is 48π square feet, what is its volume?

A) 1π ft.^{3}

B) 16π ft.^{3}

C) 32π ft.^{3}

D) 64π ft.^{3}

39. What are the zeros of $\left(\frac{g}{h}\right)(k)$ if $g(k) = -3k^2 - k$ and $h(k) = -2k - 4$?

A) $\left\{0, \frac{1}{3}\right\}$

B) $\{-2\}$

C) $\{0\}$

D) $\left\{-2, 0, \frac{1}{3}\right\}$

40. If $\triangle JKL \sim \triangle PQR$ and $JK = 10$, $KL = 18.2$, $JL = 13.4$, and $QR = 47.1$, what is the approximate perimeter of $\triangle PQR$?

A) 42

B) 80

C) 108

D) 135

Constructed Response
Work the problem and construct your response in the space provideD)

1. If $j = 4$, what is the value of $2(j - 4)^4 - j + \frac{1}{2}j$?

Write in the answer: _____

2. Fifteen DVDs are to be arranged on a shelf. 4 of the DVDs are horror films, 6 are comedies, and 5 are science fiction. In how many ways can the DVDs be arranged if DVDs of the same genre must be placed together?

Write in the answer: _____

3. A worker was paid $15,036 for 7 months of work. If he received the same amount each month, how much was he paid for the first 2 months?

Write in the answer: _____

4. If $\triangle ABD \sim \triangle DEF$ and the similarity ratio is 3:4, what is the measure of DE if $AB = 12$?

Write in the answer: _____

5. If angles a and b are congruent, what is the measurement of angle c?

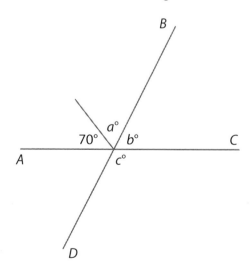

Write in the answer: _____

6. Which of the following is a solution of the given equation?

$$4(m + 4)^2 - 4m^2 + 20 = 276$$

Write in the answer: _____

7. Find the 12th term of the following sequence.

$-57, -40, -23, -6...$

Write in the answer: _____

9. If the water in a reservoir decreases every day by 4%, by how much will the water decrease over a 7-day week?

Write in the answer: _____

10. What is the approximate diagonal length of square QTSR shown in the figure below?

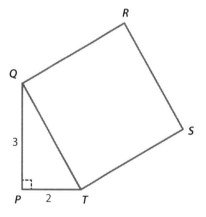

Write in the answer: _____

12. A high school cross country team sent 25 percent of its runners to a regional competition. Of these, 10 percent won medals. If 2 runners earned medals, how many members does the cross country team have?

Write in the answer: _____

8. New York had the fewest months with less than 3 inches of rain in every year except which city?

Number of Months with 3 or Fewer Than 3 Inches of Rain

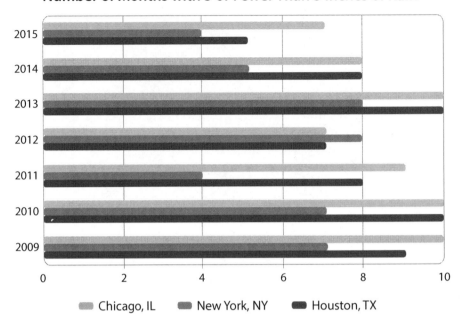

11. If the volume of a cube is 343 cubic meters, what is the cube's surface area?

Write in the answer: _____

ANSWER KEY

Multiple Choice

1. **C)** FOIL and combine like terms.

$(5 + 2i)(3 + 4i)$

$= 15 + 6i + 20i + 8i^2$

$= 15 + 6i + 20i + (8)(-1)$

$= 15 + 6i + 20i - 8$

$= \mathbf{7 + 26i}$

2. **A)** Use the formula for inversely proportional relationships to find k and then solve for s.

$sn = k$

$(65)(250) = k$

$k = 16{,}250$

$s(325) = 16{,}250$

$s = \mathbf{50}$

3. **A)** There are six digits that can be used to make up the 6-digit number: 0, 1, 2, 7, 8, and 9. However, 0 cannot be used for the first digit. Use the fundamental counting principle: $(5)(6)(6)(6)(6)(6) = \mathbf{38{,}880}$.

4. **C)** Find the slope of line b, take the negative reciprocal to find the slope of a, and test each point.

$(x_1, y_1) = (-100, 100)$

$(x_2, y_2) = (-95, 115)$

$m_b = \dfrac{115 - 100}{-95 - (-100)} = \dfrac{15}{5} = 3$

$m_a = -\dfrac{1}{3}$

$(104, 168)\!:\dfrac{100 - 168}{100 - (104)} = \dfrac{1}{3}$

$(-95, 115)\!:\dfrac{100 - 115}{100 - (-95)} = 3$

$(-112, 104)\!:\dfrac{100 - 104}{100 - (-112)} = -\dfrac{1}{3}$

$(-112, -104)\!:\dfrac{100 - (-104)}{100 - (-112)} = 17$

5. **D)** Divide the digits and subtract the exponents.

$\dfrac{7.2 \times 10^6}{1.6 \times 10^{-3}}$

$7.2 \div 1.6 = 4.5$

$6 - (-3) = 9$

$\mathbf{4.5 \times 10^9}$

6. **C)** Plug 0 in for x and solve for y.

$7y - 42x + 7 = 0$

$7y - 42(0) + 7 = 0$

$y = -1$

The y-intercept is at $\mathbf{(0, -1)}$.

7. **B)** Use the midpoint formula to find point B.

$M_x\!:\dfrac{(7 + x)}{2} = -3$

$x = -13$

$M_y: \dfrac{(12 + y)}{2} = 10$

$y = 8$

B = **(−13, 8)**

8. **A)** Variance would have a unit of hours squared, not hours.

9. **D)** Simplify using PEMDAS.

$z^3(z + 2)^2 - 4z^3 + 2$

$z^3(z^2 + 4z + 4) - 4z^3 + 2$

$z^5 + 4z^4 + 4z^3 - 4z^3 + 2$

$z^5 + 4z^4 + 2$

10. **D)** Solve each equation for y and find the equation with a power of 1.

$\sqrt[3]{y} = x \rightarrow y = x^3$

$\sqrt[3]{x} = y \rightarrow y = \sqrt[3]{x}$

$\sqrt[3]{y} = x^2 \rightarrow y = x^6$

$y = \sqrt[3]{x^3} \rightarrow$ **$y = x$**

11. **D)** Use the formula for the area of a rectangle to find the increase in its size.

$A = lw$

$A = (1.4l)(0.6w)$

$A = 0.84lw$

The new area will be 84% of the original area, a decrease of **16%**.

12. **C)** Simplify using PEMDAS.

$-(3^2) + (5 - 7)^2 - 3(4 - 8)$

$= -(3^2) + (-2)^2 - 3(-4)$

$= -9 + 4 - 3(-4)$

$= -9 + 4 + 12 =$ **7**

13. **D)** Solve the system using substitution.

$z - 2x = 14 \rightarrow z = 2x + 14$

$2z - 6x = 18$

$2(2x + 14) - 6x = 18$

$4x + 28 - 6x = 18$

$-2x = -10$

$x = 5$

$z - 2(5) = 14$

$z = 24$

14. **C)** Write a system of equations and solve using substitution.

$5a + b - 2 = 180$

$b = \dfrac{7}{8}a$

$5a + \dfrac{7}{8}a - 2 = 180$

$a =$ **30.98**

15. **D)** Set up a system of equations and solve using elimination.

f = the cost of a financial stock

a = the cost of an auto stock

$50f + 10a = 1300$

$10f + 10a = 500$

$\quad\quad 50f + 10a = 1300$

$\underline{+ -50f - 50a = -2500}$

$\quad\quad\quad -40a = -1,200$

$\quad\quad\quad\quad a = 30$

$50(30) =$ **1,500**

16. **A)** I. True: The row "25 – 35 year-olds" and the column "more than 4 hours" show a relative frequency of 0.20 or 20%.

II. True: The total relative frequency of participants who spend 2 to 4 hours on social media a day is 0.26 or 26%.

III. False: These percentages cannot be added because the "whole" is not the same. To calculate the percentage of people aged 15 – 35 who use social media less than 2 hours a day, find the total number of people in each category and divide by the total number of people in both categories.

people 15 – 25 years old spending < 2 hrs. = 0.15(200) = 30

people 25 – 35 years old spending < 2 hrs. = 0.52(200) = 104

percentage of people 15 – 35 years old spending < 2 hrs. $= \dfrac{30 + 104}{400} = 0.34 = 34\%$

IV. False: The number of people aged 35 – 45 who used social media more than 4 hours a day is 0.05(200) = 10.

17. **D)** Write a proportion and then solve for x.

$\dfrac{40}{45} = \dfrac{265}{x}$

$40x = 11,925$

$x = 298.125 \approx \mathbf{298}$

18. **A)** Use the midpoint formula to find the center of the circle and the distance formula to find its radius.

$M_x = \frac{4 + (-12)}{2} = -4$

$M_y = \frac{5 + (-11)}{2} = -3$

$M = (-4, -3)$

$r = \frac{1}{2}\sqrt{(4 - (-8))^2 + (5 - (-11))^2} = 10$

Use the center and radius to write the equation for the circle.

$(x - h)^2 + (y - k)^2 = r^2$

$\mathbf{(x + 4)^2 + (y + 3)^2 = 100}$

19. **C)** Use the equation for tangent.

$\tan 50° = \frac{x}{300}$

$x = 300(\tan 50°)$

$\mathbf{x \approx 357}$

20. **B)** Use the equation for Bernoulli trials (binomial distribution).

$P = {}_nC_r (p^r)(q^{n-r})$

$n = 10$

$r = 3$

$p = \frac{4}{36} = \frac{1}{9}$

$q = \frac{8}{9}$

$P = {}_{10}C_3 \left(\frac{1}{9}\right)^3 \left(\frac{8}{9}\right)^7 = 0.072 = \mathbf{7.2\%}$

21. **C)** Set up a proportion to find the weight of the removed wedge.

$\frac{60°}{x \text{ lb.}} = \frac{360°}{73 \text{ lb.}}$

$x \approx 12.17 \text{ lb.}$

Subtract the removed wedge from the whole to find the weight of the remaining piece.

$73 - 12.17 = \mathbf{60.83}$

22. **A)** Simplify the inequality.

$2x + 4 \geq 5x - 20 - 3x + 12$

$2x + 4 \geq 2x - 8$

$4 \geq -8$

Since the inequality is always true, the

solution is all real numbers, $(-\infty, \infty)$.

23. **B)** The axis of symmetry will be a vertical line that runs through the vertex, which is the point $(-3, 5)$. The line of symmetry is $x = -3$.

24. **C)** Use the formula for percent change.

$percent\ change = \frac{amount\ of\ change}{original\ amount}$

$= \frac{(7,375 - 7,250)}{7,250} = 0.017 = \mathbf{1.7\%}$

25. **B)** Factor the trinomial and set each factor equal to 0.

$2n^2 + 2n - 12 = 0$

$2(n^2 + n - 6) = 0$

$2(n + 3)(n - 2) = 0$

$\mathbf{n = -3}$ and $\mathbf{n = 2}$

26. **D)** Find where the denominator equals 0.

$-2x - 6 = 0$

$\mathbf{x = -3}$

27. **B)** The slope 0.0293 gives the increase in passenger car miles (in billions) for each year that passes. Muliply this value by 5 to find the increase that occurs over 5 years: $5(0.0293) = \mathbf{0.1465}$ **billion miles**.

28. **D)** There are an infinite number of points with distance four from the origin, all of which lie on a circle centered at the origin with a radius of 4.

29. Eliminate answer choices that don't match the graph.

A) Correct.

B) The graph has a negative slope while this inequality has a positive slope.

C) The line on the graph is solid, so the inequality should include the "or equal to" symbol.

D) The shading is above the line, meaning the inequality should be "y is greater than."

30. **C)** Use the rules of exponents to simplify the expression.

$$\left(\frac{4x^{-3}y^4z}{8x^{-5}y^3z^{-2}}\right)^2 = \left(\frac{x^2yz^3}{2}\right)^2 = \frac{x^4y^2z^6}{4}$$

31. **A)** Subtract $g(x)$ from $f(x)$.

$x^2 + 16x - (5x^2 + 4x + 25) = x^2 + 16x - 5x^2$
$- 4x - 25 = $ **$-4x^2 + 12x - 25$**

32. **A) False**: 350 is the median, but the median does not have to be a value in the set.

B) True: The highest value is 550, and the lowest value is 150: 550 − 150 = 400.

C) True: 450 is the third quartile (Q3), meaning 75% of the set is below that value.

D) True: The middle 50%, or interquartile range, is between Q2 = 250 and Q3 = 450.

33. **B)** The altitude creates a **30–60–90 triangle with a height of $5\sqrt{3}$.**

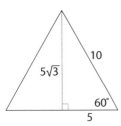

34. **B)** Multiply by the complex conjugate and simplify.

$$\frac{3+\sqrt{3}}{4-\sqrt{3}}\left(\frac{4+\sqrt{3}}{4+\sqrt{3}}\right)$$

$$= \frac{12+4\sqrt{3}+3\sqrt{3}+3}{16-4\sqrt{3}+4\sqrt{3}-3} = \frac{15+7\sqrt{3}}{13}$$

35. **D)** Split the absolute value inequality into two inequalities and simplify. Switch the inequality when making one side negative.

$\frac{x}{8} \geq 1$
$x \geq 8$

$\frac{-x}{8} \geq 1$
$\frac{x}{8} \leq -1$
$x \leq -8$

$x \leq -8$ or $x \geq 8 \rightarrow (-\infty, -8] \cup [8, \infty)$

36. **D)** Use the graph to find the number of months Chicago had less than 3 inches of rain year, and then find the average.

months with < 3 inches rain in Chicago: {7, 8, 10, 7, 9, 10, 10}

$$\frac{(7 + 8 + 10 + 7 + 9 + 10 + 10)}{7} = 8.7 \approx \mathbf{9}$$

37. **C)** Expand the original expression using the properties of logarithms.

$$\log_6\left(\frac{36}{x}\right) = \log_6(36) - \log_6(x) = \mathbf{2 - \log_6 x}$$

38. **C)** Find the height of the cylinder using the equation for surface area.

$SA = 2\pi rh + 2\pi r^2$
$48\pi = 2\pi(4)h + 2\pi(4)^2$
$h = 2$

Find the volume using the volume equation.

$V = \pi r^2 h$
$V = \pi(4)^2(2) = \mathbf{32\pi \ ft.^3}$

39. **A)** Set the numerator of the resulting rational function equal to 0 to find the zeros.

$$\left(\frac{g}{h}\right)(k) = \frac{(-3k^2 - k)}{(-2k - 4)}$$
$0 = 3k^2 - k$
$0 = k(3k - 1)$
$\mathbf{k = 0, \frac{1}{3}}$

40. **C)** Find the perimeter of $\triangle JKL$.

$P = 10 + 18.2 + 13.4 = 41.6$

Find the scale factor between the two triangles.

$$\frac{QR}{KL} = \frac{47.1}{18.2} = 2.588$$

Multiply the perimeter of $\triangle JKL$ by the scale factor to find the perimeter of $\triangle PQR$.

$(2.588)(41.6) = 107.6 \approx \mathbf{108}$

Constructed Response

1. Plug 4 in for j and simplify.

$2(j-4)^4 - j + \frac{1}{2}j$

$2(4-4)^4 - 4 + \frac{1}{2}(4) = \mathbf{-2}$

2. Use the fundamental counting principle to determine how many ways the DVDs can be arranged within each category and how many ways the 3 categories can be arranged.

ways to arrange horror $= 4! = 24$

ways to arrange comedies $= 6! = 720$

ways to arrange science fiction $= 5! = 120$

ways to arrange categories $= 3! = 6$

$(24)(720)(120)(6) = \mathbf{12,441,600}$

3. Write a proportion and then solve for x.

$\frac{15,036}{7} = \frac{x}{2}$

$7x = 30,072$

$x = \mathbf{4,296}$

4. Set up a proportion and solve.

$\frac{AB}{DE} = \frac{3}{4}$

$\frac{12}{DE} = \frac{3}{4}$

$3(DE) = 48$

$\mathbf{DE = 16}$

5. Use the two sets of linear angles to find b and then c.

$a = b$

$a + b + 70 = 180$

$2a + 70 = 180$

$a = b = 55°$

$b + c = 180°$ $55 + c = 180$

$c = \mathbf{125°}$

6. Plug each value into the equation.

$4(3+4)^2 - 4(3)^2 + 20 = 180 \neq 276$

$4(6+4)^2 - 4(6)^2 + 20 = \mathbf{276}$

$4(12+4)^2 - 4(12)^2 + 20 = 468 \neq 276$

$4(24+4)^2 - 4(24)^2 + 20 = 852 \neq 276$

7. Find the perimeter of $\triangle JKL$.

$P = 10 + 18.2 + 13.4 = 41.6$

Find the scale factor between the two triangles.

$\frac{QR}{KL} = \frac{47.1}{18.2} = 2.588$

Multiply the perimeter of $\triangle JKL$ by the scale factor to find the perimeter of $\triangle PQR$.

$(2.588)(41.6) = 107.6 \approx \mathbf{108}$

9. Use the exponential decay function. The value $\frac{y}{a}$ represents the percent of the water remaining.

$y = a(1-r)^t$

$y = (1-0.04)^7$

$y = (0.96)^7 = 0.751$

After 7 days, the new amount of water is 0.751, or 75.1% of the original amount. It has decreased by $100 - 75.1 = \mathbf{24.9\%}$.

10. Find the hypotenuse of $\triangle QPT$.

$H_1 = QT = \sqrt{3^2 + 2^2} = 3.6$

Find the diagonal of $QRST$.

$H_1 = SQ = \sqrt{3.6^2 + 3.6^2} = \mathbf{5.09}$

12. Work backwards to find the number of runners in the competition (c) and then the number of runners on the team (r).

$\frac{2}{c} = \frac{10}{100}$

$c = 20$

$\frac{20}{r} = \frac{25}{100}$

$r = \mathbf{80}$

8. In 2012, New York had more months with less than 3 inches of rain than either Chicago or Houston.

11. Use the volume to find the length of the cube's side.

$V = s^3$

$343 = s^3$

$s = 7$ m

Find the area of each side and multiply

by 6 to find the total surface area.

7(7) = 49 m

49(6) = **294 m²**

Made in the USA
Middletown, DE
04 April 2017